LIVING WITH THE LEGACY OF ABUSE

How to make your relationship work when your partner is a survivor of childhood sexual abuse

By Beverly Engel
Foreword by Robin Skynner
Introduction by Valerie Sinason

First published in the United States as
Partners in Recovery

Camden Press Limited
46 Colebrooke Row
London N1 8AF

Published in the UK 1998 by

Camden Press Ltd
46 Colebrooke Row
London N1 8AF

First published in the USA by Lowell House, Los Angeles, CA

Cover Design: Chris Hyde

Cover photograph: Antonia Deutch

Researcher /Co-ordinator: Charlie Murray

Printed and bound in England by BPC Information Ltd, Marsh Barton, Exeter, Devon

British Library Cataloguing-in-Publication Data.
A catalogue record for this book is available from the British Library.

ISBN 0 9 48491 53 1

Publishing for Change

Living with the Legacy of Abuse by Beverly Engel is the first book published in a new series we call **Publishing for Change**. Each book in the series will be part of a larger project based on a book's subject.

The primary aim of the **Partners Project** based on Ms Engel's book will be to increase awareness among therapists, voluntary agencies and the public in general of the relationship problems faced by adult survivors of childhood abuse and in particular the problems faced by the survivor's partner.

The **Partners Project** will include:

- A national conference organised and sponsored by Camden Press for therapists and other professionals on the relationship problems of adult survivors of sexual abuse.

- A research project which will provide group therapy to six couples where one of the partners is a survivor of abuse. The information generated by this project will be made available without cost to professionals in the field of child abuse.

- Training seminars for therapists and voluntary services dealing with survivors and their families.

- Information and assistance to partners wanting to set up self-help groups.

Publishing for Change is made possible by funding from the Camden Graphics Trust and the time and energy contributed by many individuals who want to do something for those **Living with the Legacy of Abuse**. For further information regarding this and future **Publishing for Change** projects, write to Camden Press, 46 Colebrooke Row, London N1 8AF.

The Author

Beverly Engel is an internationally recognised expert in the field of abuse as well as a noted author, workshop leader, psychotherapist and sex therapist with over twenty three years experience as a licensed Marriage, Family and Child Counsellor.

Ms Engel is the author of nine books in her field, including *The Right to Innocence*: Healing the Trauma of Childhood Sexual Abuse and her most recent work *Families in Recovery*.

Author's Dedication and Acknowledgements

This book is dedicated to all of the partners and friends who have supported and encouraged me throughout my recovery. I wish to thank Janice Gallagher and Mary Nadler who helped to make my books the best they can be with their excellent editing and valuable suggestions.

Publisher's Note

I would like to thank friends and colleagues who have contributed to this project through their advice, support and encouragement and especially Peter Allez, Jasmine Blanche, Susan Kaye, Dr Vera Pettitt, Sheila Stephens, Paula Wakefield, Dr. Harold Behr and Vickie Ross. A special thanks to Charlie Murray.

Contents

PART III:
SPECIAL ISSUES FOR INTIMATE PARTNERS

Foreword

by Robin Skynner

For too long child sexual abuse has been viewed, often with morbid curiosity, only at the extremes of the spectrum of that experience. Patients fitting the description of adult survivors were perceived as bending the ear of the therapist with prurient accounts of what a parent had done, or allowed to be done to them. Their problems were nailed firmly to the mast of abuse and too often accepted without question by therapists.Most experienced and competent therapists deal with these patients and seek the welfare of the family as a whole. But a few irresponsible ones seem to take an almost prurient interest in the details of abuse and bring the profession into disrepute.

Then the inevitable backlash - the other end of the spectrum - with recollections of sexual abuse by therapy patients described as "false memory syndrome". Newspapers splashed stories of psychotherapists taken to court by allegedly abusive fathers for "putting these ideas into the patient's head". This attack eventually widened to include not just the competence of individual therapists, but therapy itself.

In the public domain we also see these extremes. The scandal of massive state intervention, without adequate evidence, often unjustly separated children from their families. At the other extreme, the scandal in North Wales where vulnerable and defenceless children in care were sexually abused, often by the very persons charged with their care and protection.

Beverly Engel's book attracted me at once because she does not operate at the extremes. Rather, she writes plainly of the effect childhood sexual abuse has on adult relationships. Her account of the problems likely to be faced in such a relationship is very accurate. Her suggestions as to how these difficulties might be approached, whether in the sexual relationship itself or in other aspects of the couple's interactions, are highly relevant and likely to assist any couple in which childhood sexual abuse has caused, or is likely to cause problems.

I agree entirely with the view expressed by Ms Engel that the so-called "healthy" partner is also likely to have experienced some kind of abuse in their childhood. As I explain in *Families and How to Survive Them*, couples who are attracted to each other have similar family backgrounds. But the experience, say, of physical abuse or even emotional invasiveness may help someone better understand the feelings of the partner with a sexually abusive history. Perhaps it also makes them the ideal person to assist their partner to overcome the fears and failings which their early life has left them. Professionals working with victims of child sexual abuse should find this book equally valuable in giving an insight into the feelings such experiences generate and in suggesting new ideas about ways of reducing guilt and low self-esteem with which such people are left.

There is much pleasure in reading a book which so skilfully deals with these painful issues, to a point where I believe that many people will be adequately helped by working through it with their partners, and so will not necessarily need psychotherapy. However, for those attending for psychotherapy as couples, the book forms an ideal accompaniment. I recommend it highly to all colleagues, whether they have a special interest in this field or not.

Introduction

by Valerie Sinason

After the second world war there was an enormous wave of hope for the future. Children were to experience a proper childhood free from external catastrophe and picture-books such as the "Janet and John" series provided semi-delusional middle class images of safe, contented affluent family life with two loving parents. Only since the 1980s have we had the societal strength to recognise how damaged we are as a community. Sexual abuse is the only crime that is easier to disclose several years later. Hence, whilst as many as 1% of English children are the subjects of case conferences on all forms of abuse(Browne, 1989), when it comes to adults (Baker & Duncan, 1985, Hall,1985) it is estimated that 8% of men and 12-16% of women have experienced some kind of sexual abuse in childhood.

If we took the most conservative estimates of a 5% experience of abuse, in a country of 60 million people we are looking at 3 million people. If we consider the massive media and political interventions on possibly infected food that has harmed under a hundred people and imagine what the outcry would be if 3 million people were infected by BSE or salmonella we can see how intolerable it is for us as a society to consider the extent of abuse.

This minimum number of 3 million citizens does not exist in isolation either. They are in families, in social networks, in relationships. The consequences of their childhood violation has powerful inter-connecting effects on others. When you find the man or woman you love has experienced betrayal on such a profound level you can feel, in a smaller way, the feelings of helplessness, rage and violation that they suffered.

What help is there for you if you are a partner? Egeland (1988) amongst others found that those who managed to break the cycle of abuse had received some form of help that enabled them to maintain stable relationships. Browne (1993) points out that "whether it was a relative, a therapist or a social worker, somewhere in their life history was someone who listened, believed and expressed empathy and understanding about their experiences".

Belief from a friend or partner is a necessary pre-requisite for recovery. Varley (1984) in a study of female learning-disabled abuse victims who were disbelieved found that over half were vulnerable to psychotic breakdown. Whilst a smaller proportion of the non-learning-disabled abused who are disbelieved have a psychotic breakdown, their recovery is hindered in other ways.

Abuse constitutes a painful interface between private grief and public legal processes. Whilst the law cannot and should not believe anything until it is proven, a partner or friend is not a Judge and Court. However, the fact that an offence has occurred means that partners have to deal with the emotional consequences of complex public processes in addition to the other aspects of privately dealing with a partner's vulnerabilities.

Outside of the professional network, what help is there for that crucial "someone" who needs to listen and believe? Within the UK there are now many useful clinical textbooks on child abuse and its consequences. These are for health service professionals. There are also story books for abused children to allow them the opportunity to reflect on their experience through a transitional space. Increasingly, there have been self-help books from a range of theoretical and clinical bases for survivors. However, what is there for the survivor's partner, the most important potential helper of all?

Bob Borzello, Director of Camden Press, has a long history of recognising major societal areas that are taboo and where the help provided is inadequate. He has, for example, campaigned against racism in the media for many years. He realised a while ago there was a major gap in the abuse literature and said "I finally found what was missing" when he came across an American book by Beverly Engel, a marriage, family and child counsellor who has specialised in working with adult children from abusive families. She is also the founder and director for the Centre for Adult Survivors of Sexual Abuse (CASSA).

Engel sees her book as a guide for Prosurvivors, her term for the partner of a survivor (regardless of whether the partner is also a survivor), as well as helpful for the survivor who might need to know the impact his/her patterns are having on partners, whether heterosexual and homosexual. The book is clearly written and divides into three parts : what you need to know in order to help a survivor, coping with the phases of recovery and special issues for intimate partners.

In the first part Ms Engel takes the reader through the myths and facts of abuse, through the processes of facing the truth about abuse, dealing with the anger, facing the perpetrator internally or externally, resolving family relationships, learning self-care and finally self-forgiveness. Ms Engel throughout respects the need of the survivor to have choice and she has no hidden agenda in her writing. For example, in the controversial area of how the adult survivor should deal with her abuser she presents as equal choices an internal ability to confront the abuser in one's own mind (which she calls "indirect" confrontation whether accomplished with a partner or a professional) or an external one in which the survivor writes, phones or speaks to their abuser. She clearly shows the dangers of each method.

In the second part, coping with the stages of recovery, Ms Engel takes the survivor's partner through the stages, processes and primitive responses involved in recovery. The first step is confronting the truth which means coping with the disclosure, when you can not believe it, when you feel angry the survivor did not disclose earlier, when you cannot understand how they let it happen and finally, when the perpetrator was an attachment figure. She also takes the reader through painful essential prejudiced questions that reveal the way we, as friends of the survivors also internalise the abuser's propaganda and blame the victim - why didn't they tell?, why did they go back?, what if they got pleasure from it?, what if they were old enough to know?, were they in some way asking for it? We then look at the processes involved in anger, family relationships, self-discovery and self-care.

Self-Discovery and Self-Care for the survivor's partner are very much aimed at "Physician, heal thyself". The partner is asked very openly, courteously but nevertheless painfully to consider the possibility of their co-dependence, their need for their partner's disturbance. Useful advice is given.

Part three is devoted to special issues for intimate partners and deals with the damage done to the sexual aspect of relationships through childhood abuse. Engel provides useful definitions of common sexual difficulties as well as practical exercises.

Importantly, she tackles the dangers involved in sexual play that can mirror the past abuse scenario.

Her final chapter, "Should you stay or should you leave?", continues offering honest discussion on a fraught topic. There is no Pollyannaesque idea that through reading the book couples can or should maintain their relationship.

Engel does not simplify the emotional task of being a survivor or a survivor's partner. In simple non-technical language she explicitly enumerates the problems that both face. Neither is she doom laden and hopeless. In the best tradition of good self-help books she provides honest, well-researched commentary and advice whilst pointing the need for professional input where the book starts the process of recovery but more is needed. This book will be of use to survivors and their partners as well as to professionals.

Clinicians meet with a biased sample consisting as it does of those who come to us. In the community are vast numbers who have been attempting to heal themselves (often successfully) as well as those who are most hurt but ashamed to gain help. This book, filling as it does such a major gap in the literature, will hopefully point those who need it towards therapy and counselling as well as allowing others to complete their recovery with those they love and trust the best.

An extra note on Memory for UK readers

Whilst the survivor has to be believed, both the survivor and his/her partner needs to bear in mind that those who have suffered the greatest trauma can have more distortions in their memory (Sinason 1998). In other words, when abuse has been particularly traumatic, it is difficult to discover where between the real abuse and the fantasy distortion of that abuse the truth lies. This means empathically responding to all the survivor says but bearing in mind for both of you that there can be some distortion. There is likely to be most distortion the further back the memories go (ie under 4 years old). Equally, memory that comes suddenly that the survivor has not before been consciously aware of is open to distortion as are memories that come through hypnosis. Unfortunately it is only occasionally that the worst memories are the distortions (Sinason 1993). A further by-product of the interest in False Memory in the USA and the UK is to make it clearer that abusers are likely to have a worse memory than their victims and in certain cases genuinely have no memory of abusing.

Baker, A W & Duncan, SP (1985) Child sexual abuse: a study of prevalence in Britain.
Child Abuse & Neglect 8 (4): 457-67
Browne, KD (1993) Violence in the family and its links to child abuse in Baillliere's *Clinical Paediatrics International Practice and Research, Child Abuse*, eds Hobbs C.J. & Wynne, J.M. Bailliere Tindall, London.
Egeland B (1988) Breaking the cycle of abuse: implications for prediction and Intervention in Browne, K.D., Davies, C & Stratton, P (eds) *Early Prediction and Prevention of Child Abuse*, pp 87-102, Chichester, Wiley.
Hall, RE (1985) *Ask any woman*, London, Falling Wall Press.
Sinason, V (1993) *Treating Survivors of Satanist Abuse*. Routledge.
Sinason, V (1998) *Memory in Dispute*, Karnac Books.
Variety, CK (1984) Schizophreniform psychoses in mentally retarded adolescent girls following sexual assault, *American Journal of Psychiatry* 141 (4): 593-55.

Valerie Sinason is a Consultant Research Psychotherapist at St George's Hospital Medical School, a Consultant Child Psychotherapist at the Tavistock Clinic and a poet.

Preface

TO THE PROSURVIVOR

My first book, *The Right to Innocence: Healing the Trauma of Childhood Sexual Abuse*, was published in 1988. In the few years since then, there has been a tremendous amount of media coverage about this issue, and adults who were sexually abused as children have flocked to therapists and joined recovery groups in droves. Original estimates of the number of people thought to have been sexually molested as children have proved to be too low. Today, most experts agree that at least one in three adults, both male and female, were sexually abused as children. (Some experts even believe that 50 percent of American women were sexually abused as children.)

As a natural outgrowth of the fact that so many survivors are seeking help, there is another entire population of people who need, and are seeking, help. These are the prosurvivors. *Prosurvivor* is the term commonly used by those in the recovery field to describe someone—a mate or lover, or a friend—who is in a supportive relationship with a survivor and who wants to support and encourage the survivor through the recovery process. Although they feel supportive, many prosurvivors are being adversely affected by the sexual abuse the survivor sustained. Those affected the most are the mates of survivors, who are influenced daily by the survivor's moods, fears, outbursts, and lack of trust. Since more and more survivors are now either remembering the abuse for the first time or feeling more free to talk openly about it, there are more and more people who are discovering that they are married to or intimately involved with a survivor of childhood sexual abuse.

Many therapists report an increase in the number of prosurvivors who are entering therapy to understand what the survivor needs from them and/or to seek support for their own problems in the relationship. However, until now there have been no books written expressly for prosurvivors, offering them the same kind of support and information that survivors are now able to get.

Originally, I had planned to write this book for *anyone* who was close to a survivor, including parents and other members of the original family. However, I have decided to focus instead only on the mates, lovers, and friends of survivors, since these three groups share similar concerns. Members of the survivor's original family often have a separate set of concerns, and in my next book I will specifically address the needs of family members.

I have written *Partners in Recovery* to bring to you, the prosurvivor, the benefits of my multilevel experience—to offer you my insights as a survivor, my empathy and understanding as a prosurvivor, and my expertise as a therapist.

As a survivor, I have had the fortunate experience of having a partner who supported me through the different phases of my recovery, and who worked on understanding that many of my behaviors were symptoms of my early childhood trauma. This support and understanding encouraged me to stay open to my feelings and to not judge myself even when I sometimes acted in strange or unfamiliar ways.

I have also been the partner or friend of several survivors. Because I did not know that they were survivors, I viewed behaviors that I now recognize as long-term effects of childhood sexual abuse (for example, difficulty in trusting) as personal affronts to me. I thought partners who needed space and alone time were simply rejecting and uncaring. Looking back on these relationships, I can see now that I acted insensitively and unkindly toward people who were genuinely suffering.

Finally, as a therapist who has worked with both survivors and prosurvivors for the past 17 years, I have had yet another type of opportunity to see that both have unique problems that need to be attended to.

Understanding that there are almost as many males as females who have been sexually abused as children, I have written this book for partners of both sexes. However, since it is difficult to work with the pronouns *he* and *she*, I will primarily use the feminine to represent the survivor and the masculine to represent the prosurvivor, since up to this point there are more known female survivors than male and more females seeking help. When at all possible, I will use *he* to represent the survivor, and I will give examples of both male and female survivors.

By the same token, because many survivors are homosexual or bisexual, the use of *he* for the prosurvivor and *she* for the survivor will not always fit. Once again, I ask your indulgence. I have given many examples in the book of female-female relationships and male-male relationships in order to facilitate as wide a reader identification base as possible.

Finally, I also want to make it clear that many prosurvivors are also themselves survivors of childhood sexual abuse (and may or may not be aware of the abuse). This book therefore applies to you as either a prosurvivor or a survivor.

It is not uncommon for survivors to enter into relationships with other survivors. In order for a two-survivor relationship to be successful, both partners must work on their own recoveries. While it will be difficult for both of you to be going through so much at the same time, the positive aspects of two-survivor relationships are that you are more likely to understand what each other is experiencing, and you can share resources.

Partners in Recovery will help you if you are in any of the following situations:

- ➤ Your partner or friend has just discovered that she is a survivor of childhood sexual abuse, and you'd like to know how you can help her.
- ➤ Your partner or friend has known for some time that she is a survivor but has just told you about it. You feel shocked, confused, and angry, and you don't know what to do with your feelings.
- ➤ You have suspected for some time that your partner or friend is a survivor, but she herself seems unaware of it. You'd like to know how you can help her to admit it to herself.
- ➤ Your partner or friend recognizes that she is a survivor but feels it has nothing to do with her life now or with her relationship with you. You suspect that a lot of her problems in and out of the relationship may stem from the abuse.
- ➤ You're just getting involved with someone who was sexually abused as a child, and you'd like to know what to expect.
- ➤ You and your partner are having a lot of problems, and you are desperate to save the relationship.
- ➤ You and your partner are having sexual problems. You'd like to know just how much the sexual abuse contributes to the problems, and what you and your partner can do to make things better.
- ➤ You've just separated from a survivor, and you want to know if there was something you could have done differently.
- ➤ Both you and your partner or friend are survivors, and you want to know how you can work together to be there for each other.

TO THE SURVIVOR

This book will help your partner or friend to understand more of what you are going through during your recovery process. With this added understanding, the prosurvivor will be far less likely to be judgmental, critical, and impatient with you, and more willing to go through the recovery process with you.

Reading *Partners in Recovery* yourself will help you to understand what the prosurvivor will be going through during your recovery process, and just how much you can fairly ask of him. It will help you to be aware that the prosurvivor may react in certain ways not because he doesn't love you or care about you, but because childhood sexual abuse is such a terribly uncomfortable subject and/or because he is responding to his own past and his own family scenario.

Survivors need to understand that prosurvivors are only human and are therefore imperfect. Survivors tend to look for someone to rescue them, who will be all-giving and ever-understanding. But even the most patient and caring of people have limits, saturation points, and needs. Total self-sacrifice is not healthy.

Prosurvivors tend to be codependents, or people who put aside their own needs to care for others. Because of this tendency, many prosurvivors will need encouragement from you, the survivor, to make sure they take care of themselves and lead their own lives during the recovery process instead of becoming overly involved with your difficulties. This will, in turn, give you the time and space you will so desperately need during the recovery process. By understanding how codependency works and what some of the common pitfalls are, you and your partner can work together to make the relationship work while each of you works toward your own healing.

PART I

What You Need to Know in Order to Help a Survivor

Chapter One

Partners in Recovery

Every survivor of childhood sexual abuse desperately needs someone who will stand by her throughout the recovery process. That process can be very difficult and may sometimes take up to five years, or even longer. Survivors who have the loving support of a partner are able to recover in less time than those who have no such support. By learning how to be a partner in recovery, you have the opportunity to lighten the load of the survivor, who is likely overburdened with pain, fear, anger, and guilt.

As much as you want to help and as much as you empathize with the survivor's struggle, being a partner in recovery is no easy task. It is easy to feel overwhelmed when it comes to the issue of childhood sexual abuse. You may become overwhelmed with the immense amount of anger and pain that the survivor continues to feel, with your own feelings of pain and anger over knowing that someone you care about was violated in such a terrible way, with your aching desire to help the survivor, and with the feelings that are stirred up in you about your own childhood. You may also experience a terrible sense of helplessness: You want to help, but you just don't know what to do.

The recovery process will require your utmost patience. Because survivors are in such pain, they are not always the easiest people in the world to get along with, *especially* during the recovery process. At times their pain will feel unbearable to them, and consequently you will also find it hard to take. There will be times when the survivor will seem unreasonable, when she will take her anger out on you, and when she will have a difficult time believing that you care about her, no matter how hard you try to support her. At times, you may feel tempted to throw in the towel.

This book is as much about learning to take care of yourself in the relationship as it is about learning how to be supportive of the survivor. The closer and more intimate the relationship, the more you will feel the survivor's pain, anger, and withdrawal, and the more changes you yourself will undergo.

Above all, you must understand that it is not your responsibility to rescue or "save" your partner, no matter how helpless and damaged she appears to be. She is the only one who is going to be able to save herself; she is the one who must make a commitment to her recovery and be willing to go through the pain to the other side. You can be a supportive partner, walking along beside her on her road to recovery, or you can patiently wait for her at the end of the road—but you cannot walk down the road for her.

There will be times when you will need to retreat in order to nurture yourself, when you must say no in order to enforce your own boundaries and limits, and when you must choose yourself over the survivor.

You will need all the support you can get as you work to support and cope with a survivor. I recommend that in addition to reading this book, mates, lovers, and even friends join a prosurvivors' group. In such a group you will have the chance to talk with other prosurvivors about your concerns and experiences, receiving much-needed support and suggestions on getting through difficult times.

Although there are not a lot of prosurvivors' groups established, there may be one in your area. Ask your friend or partner to ask at her next survivors' group meeting whether a prosurvivors' group has been set up. She could also ask her therapist for a referral to a prosurvivor's group. If you have already looked for help and have been unable to find it, you may want to encourage your local Alcoholics Anonymous or other Twelve-Step program to consider starting a prosurvivors' group.

It is inevitable that the relationship you have with the survivor will go through many changes. The person you thought you knew so well may sometimes act like a stranger, doing things you never would have expected and behaving in ways that you might not approve of. The survivor may become uninterested in things you once had in common or may take up new interests that you do not share. She or he may go through long periods of withdrawal from the relationship, either by not wanting to have the same amount of contact or by becoming uncommunicative. During the recovery process, the survivor may go through periods when she may not want to be close to anyone, not even those she loves very dearly. She may push you away if you try to comfort her, refuse to have any physical contact with you whatsoever, or even refuse to talk to you. On the other hand, there may be times when she is extremely needy and even childlike. She may want you to hold her but not be sexual, give to her but not give back to you. Or, she may alternate between being very needy and wanting a lot of closeness, only to change seemingly overnight and not want to be close to you at all.

Fortunately, the chances of your relationship remaining intact are increased considerably if both of you have a good idea of just what the recovery process entails. Unless you know what to expect, your partner or friend's recovery process can be extremely confusing and unsettling for you. Prosurvivors who are unprepared for the inevitable changes in the relationship may think that the relationship is falling apart, not realizing that it may simply need to get worse before it gets better. For this reason, it will be important for both you and your partner to learn all you can about the recovery process. Later in this book I will lead you step by step through the recovery process, explaining how the survivor will react during each phase of recovery and how you can best provide support.

HOW CAN I HELP BOTH OF US?

Partners in Recovery is divided into three parts. Part One begins with an information section, providing important facts about childhood sexual abuse, answering many of your most pressing questions about the subject, and helping you to separate the myths from the truth. In addition, Part One spells out exactly what the survivor needs from you, from the importance of believing what she tells you, to understanding that you must earn the survivor's trust. Last, but certainly not least, Part One outlines each stage of recovery and tells you exactly what it is that you can expect during the recovery process.

Part Two will discuss how you are likely to be affected during each of the survivor's phases of recovery, and will explain what you need to do for yourself in order to cope with the survivor's behavior during each stage.

Part Three, entitled Special Issues for Intimate Partners, is devoted mostly to the sexual problems encountered by survivors in their relationships. The most common sexual concerns of both survivors and prosurvivors are discussed, as well as solutions to these problems. Part Three also covers the issues of power and the misuse of power in a relationship with a survivor, and offers a description of what constitutes abusive behavior. The concluding chapter will help you to determine whether you should continue or leave your relationship with a survivor. Both this last chapter and the previous chapter on Power Plays are also helpful for friends of survivors.

Prosurvivors need help on a multitude of levels in order to understand and cope with the survivor and her recovery process. You may need help with your own denial so that you will believe the survivor when she tells her story, help with your anger toward the perpetrator so you don't interfere with the survivor's recovery, and help in learning coping skills to help you weather the recovery period. You will also need help in learning to cope with the rejection you will likely feel as the survivor necessarily spends more and more time focusing on her recovery. Intimate partners will need help as well in dealing with the rejection they will often feel when the survivor wants sex less often, or even not at all.

Prosurvivors need to know how to be supportive without interfering with the survivor's recovery. No matter how well-meaning they are, prosurvivors may say and do things that hamper rather than benefit the survivor. For example, giving advice to a survivor is not a good idea. It may come across as disapproval; moreover, it may actually be countertherapeutic to the person recovering. For instance, you may not approve of the survivor's staying away from her family of origin for a while, yet this may be the healthiest thing she can do.

Survivors need to know that their anger, pain, and fear are natural, healthy responses to a devastating experience. They need to experience all of their emotions, and to feel free to express those emotions without being judged, criticized, or made to feel as though they are crazy, just feeling sorry for themselves, or weak. The prosurvivor may not understand the amount of anger a survivor feels or that she or he needs to be able to ventilate this anger in a constructive way. Because many people feel threatened by anger and believe it should be repressed, survivors may be criticized for being so angry—thus reinforcing their own doubts about it. One of the best things you, the prosurvivor, can do for a survivor is to let her know that she has a right to be angry about the sexual abuse.

In addition to providing loving support, encourage your mate, lover, or friend to join a survivors' group or to begin therapy, if she hasn't already done so. While most survivors are not suicidal, those who threaten to kill themselves or who seem to be self-destructive to a point where they are endangering their lives or the lives of others need professional help as soon as possible.

If it is affordable, the combination of individual and group therapy with a licensed therapist will offer the survivor the optimum opportunity for recovery. Some survivors may need to see an individual therapist twice a week in addition to having group therapy once a week, if at all possible.

It can be threatening to you to have your partner enter therapy, because you will not know what kinds of changes she will be making. Frequently, prosurvivors fear that the survivor will change so much that she will no longer want to be in the relationship. This is especially true when the survivor has been overly dependent upon her partner because of her low self-esteem.

While it may be difficult to let your partner go and to risk that she will come back, it is a courageous and loving thing for you to do. Many relationships are strengthened and improved after the survivor seeks help—and those that aren't probably were not going to work out, anyway.

SOME ESSENTIAL TERMS

Before you begin your journey, it's important for you to be familiar with the terms most commonly used in discussing childhood sexual abuse.

Sexual Abuse—*This term includes any action on the part of an adult or an older child toward a child that is intended to sexually stimulate either the older person or the child.*

Child Molestation—*This term is used interchangeably with* ***sexual abuse.***

Incest—*The most common form of child sexual abuse, incest is any sexual contact between a child or adolescent and a person who is closely related or perceived to be related, such as a parent, sibling, cousin, uncle or aunt, grandparent, stepparent, or the live-in partner of a parent. Sometimes the definition of incest is extended to include sexual abuse by any person in a position of authority or responsibility over the child.*

Survivor—*This term is used to refer to a person who survived an abusive or neglectful childhood.* ***Survivor*** *is used instead of* ***victim*** *in order to make clear that the person does not have to continue to be a victim, and can instead identify himself or herself with all other survivors of traumatic experiences.*

Prosurvivor—*This term refers to anyone who is a caring supporter of a survivor. Prosurvivors can include mates, lovers, friends, family members, and counselors.*

Perpetrator—*This term refers to the sexual abuser or molester. Experts in the sexual abuse field have adopted this word from law-enforcement terminology in order to emphasize that childhood sexual abuse is, indeed, a crime.*

Abuser—*Some people prefer to use this word instead of* ***perpetrator*** *because it can be more descriptive and clear. I will use the two interchangeably throughout the book.*

Offender—*This term is also used interchangeably with* ***perpetrator*** *and* ***abuser.***

Silent Partner—*A silent partner can be anyone who knew, or should have known, that the sexual abuse was occurring, or who made it possible for the perpetrator to abuse the child by failing to protect, supervise, or nurture the child properly. Most commonly, it is used when discussing father/daughter or mother/son incest and refers to the parent who did not commit the abuse. The use of this term implies that both parents were actually in a partnership concerning the abuse, no matter how unconscious this may have been.*

Becoming a partner in recovery to a survivor of childhood sexual abuse can be one of the most rewarding journeys you can make. You will not only be helping someone you love, but you will also be discovering a great deal about yourself and learning to communicate more clearly and honestly. In the next chapter, you will learn exactly what the survivor in your life needs from you, and how you can go about giving it.

Chapter Two

What Does the Survivor Need from You?

To both support and cope with a survivor, you will need to be aware of what the survivor needs from you. You can then decide whether you are willing and able to meet these needs. Survivors are not always aware of exactly what they want, and even when they are they may have difficulty in communicating their needs clearly and openly. The following guidelines cover the basic needs the survivor has in relation to you, the prosurvivor, as she recovers. To best help her, you will need to:

1. *Learn all you can about sexual abuse and the healing process.*
2. *Believe what the survivor tells you.*
3. *Allow the survivor time and space to express her anger.*
4. *Allow the survivor to blame others for awhile.*
5. *Allow the survivor time and space to express her pain.*
6. *Respect the time and space it takes to heal.*
7. *Understand that you will have to earn the survivor's trust.*
8. *Don't try to rescue the survivor or do her healing for her.*

LEARN ALL YOU CAN ABOUT SEXUAL ABUSE AND THE HEALING PROCESS

The best way to support a survivor in recovery is to become aware of what she is going through. This will keep you from misjudging her and from being impatient and critical. It will also help you to avoid blaming her for the abuse or minimizing the trauma she endured. Unless you were also sexually abused as a child, you will never completely understand, of course. But the more you are willing to listen to the survivor as she tells you about her experience, the more you read about the problem, the more you will come to understand. One of the ways of gaining understanding is to read some of the many books written on the subject of adult survivors of sexual abuse. (A complete listing of such books is provided at the back of this book.) While I can't possibly tell you here everything you need to know about childhood sexual abuse, I can help you to gain a basic understanding.

Sexual abuse is one of the most devastating traumas a child can experience. There are many long-term effects of such abuse, but the one most often emphasized is that child sexual abuse robs its victims of their innocence and childhood, their trust, and their self-esteem.

It robs them of their innocence by introducing them to adult sexuality before they are capable of coping with it. It robs them of their childhood by making little "pseudo-adults" out of them, forcing them to face the cruel injustices of life at too early an age. Childhood sexual abuse can also rob a child of one or both of her parents. If the abuser is a parent, the child can never look at that parent in the same way again. And it often creates a wedge between the child and the nonoffending parent as well because the child feels guilty and unlovable and is forced to keep a secret from that parent.

Sexual abuse robs children of their trust both in others and in themselves. If the perpetrator is someone they care about, they feel betrayed and unable to ever again trust someone they love. The abuse also causes them to feel betrayed by themselves and their own bodies, because they probably did not defend themselves and because their bodies reacted to the stimuli while being violated.

Most important, sexual abuse robs children of their self-esteem. Children who are sexually violated tend to blame themselves, turning their anger at the perpetrator against themselves until they are full of self-hatred. Children who are abused by a parent or by some other relative or loved one are especially prone to self-blame, since children have a particularly difficult time recognizing that someone they love can do bad things. Instead, they find it easier to see themselves as bad, thus protecting their image of the parent as being all good. Sexual abuse causes children to feel like "damaged goods." They feel dirty, evil, and rotten.

An effective way of gaining understanding about the survivor's dilemma is to work on dispelling any of the common myths about sexual abuse that you may have accepted as being true. Among the many myths that exist, those that I have chosen to explode here are the most common.

MYTH #1

Childhood sexual abuse involves intercourse by an adult with a child. If there is no penetration, the act is not sexual abuse.

First of all, not all sexual abuse is perpetrated by adults. In *The Secret Trauma*, Diana Russell's study of female incest victims, 26 percent of the cases involved perpetrators who were under eighteen years of age, and 15 percent of the incest perpetrators were less than five years older than their victims. More and more cases of sexual abuse by an older child toward a younger or weaker child are being reported every day.

Sexual contact between children is often misunderstood as being just normal sex play. But normal sex play and exploration occurs *only* between those of the same age, sexual experience, and power. For example, when two consenting children of the same age "play doctor," this is likely to represent normal sexual experimentation, while sexual activity between a child of 9 and an adolescent of 13 is considered sexual abuse.

Second, many forms of sexual abuse do not involve intercourse or any kind of penetration. Below is an abbreviated version of a list that originally appeared in *Handbook of Clinical Intervention in Child Sexual Abuse*, by Suzanne M. Sgroi. The list contains many of the types of sexual abuse involving children of either sex:

Nudity. *The adult parades around the house nude in front of all or some of the family members.*

Disrobing. *The adult disrobes in front of the child, generally when the child and the adult are alone.*

Genital exposure. *The adult exposes his or her genitals to the child.*

Observation of the child. *The adult surreptitiously or overtly watches the child undress, bathe, excrete, or urinate.*

Kissing. *The adult kisses the child in a lingering or intimate way.*

Fondling. *The adult fondles the child's breasts, abdomen, genital area, inner thighs, or buttocks. The child may similarly fondle the adult at his or her request.*

Masturbation. *The adult masturbates while the child observes; the adult observes the child masturbating; the adult and child masturbate each other (mutual masturbation).*

Fellatio. *The adult male has the child fellate him, or the adult male or female fellates the child.*

Cunnilingus. *This type of oral-genital contact requires either the child to place his or her mouth and/or tongue on the vulva or in the vaginal area of an adult female, or the adult to place his or her mouth and/or tongue on the vulva or in the vaginal area of the female child.*

Digital (finger) penetration of the anus or rectal opening. *Perpetrators may also thrust objects such as crayons or pencils into the opening.*

Penile penetration of the anus or rectal opening.

Digital (finger) penetration of the vagina. *Other objects may also be inserted.*

"Dry intercourse." *This is a slang term describing an interaction in which the adult rubs his penis against the child's genital-rectal area or inner thighs or buttocks.*

Penile penetration of the vagina.

If any of these acts took place in infancy, childhood, or adolescence with someone older, then sexual abuse occurred. Of equal importance is any indirect or direct sexual suggestion made by an adult toward a child. This is called *approach behavior* or *covert sexual abuse*. It can include sexual looks, innuendos, or suggestive gestures. Even if the adult never engaged in touching or took any overt sexual action, the child picks up these projected sexual feelings. Closely related to covert sexual abuse is emotional sexual abuse where one or both parents in a dysfunctional marriage or a lonely single parent bonds inappropriately with one of their children. When a parent uses their child to meet their emotional needs, the relationship can easily become sexualized and romanticized.

Childhood sexual abuse can also include verbal sexual abuse, where the adult or older child talks to the child in an inappropriate, provocative way, using sexual innuendos, sexual name-calling, foul language, and the telling of dirty jokes. The showing of pornographic materials to a child is also considered sexually abusive as is using the child to make pornographic material.

Keep in mind that it is the *intention* of the adult or older child while engaging in certain acts, such as nudity, disrobing, observation of the child, that determines whether the act is actually sexually abusive. If an adult watches a child bathe, for example, but does so in a nonsexual way that does not upset the child, it may not be sexual abuse. But if the adult becomes sexually aroused while watching, it is definitely sexual abuse.

MYTH #2

Sexual contact with a child doesn't really cause any damage to the child as long as there is no violence or pain, or if it happens only once.

While the list under Myth #1 seems to increase in severity, *all* types of sexual abuse can be emotionally and psychologically damaging to a child for a lifetime, whether or not it was repeated. There is always emotional damage and pain, much of it caused by the child's feeling of betrayal by someone he or she trusted and/or cared about. Foisting sexuality upon a child too early is abusive, and it is still abuse even in the complete absence of physical pain.

There are many long-term effects of childhood sexual abuse. Not everyone who was sexually abused as a child suffers from every problem listed under the following broad categories, but most suffer from all of the symptoms listed as broad categories.

Damage to Self-Esteem and Self-Image. *Feeling that one is ugly inside; feelings of worthlessness; a tendency to over-apologize; feelings of being stupid, a failure, a loser; tremendous guilt feelings and feelings of shame; a tendency to blame oneself for whatever goes wrong; a tendency to sabotage success; a tendency to be victimized by others; feelings of helplessness.*

Relationship Problems. *Difficulty trusting others; a tendency to be distant and aloof; a tendency to get involved with destructive people who are abusive physically, emotionally, or sexually; a lack of empathy or concern for others; a deep sense of isolation; difficulty with physical affection; secrecy, evasiveness, and a tendency to either withhold information from others or to tell all; a tendency to help others to the point of not taking care of themselves; difficulties with authority figures; difficulties communicating desires, thoughts, and feelings to others; difficulty receiving from others.*

Sexual Problems. *Lack of sexual desire; inability to enjoy sex or to have an orgasm; sexual dysfunction; inability to enjoy certain types of sexuality; problems with sexual identity; promiscuity; attraction to "illicit" sexual activities, such as pornography and prostitution; anger and disgust at any public (or media) display of affection, sexuality, nudity, or partial nudity; a tendency to be sexually manipulative; sexual addiction.*

Emotional Problems. *Intense anger and rage that sometimes burst out unexpectedly; mood swings, ranging from deep depression to extreme anxiety; chronic depression, dissociation, or "splitting off," from oneself, including time blockages and feelings of numbness in various parts of the body; extreme fears or phobias; sleep disturbances; addiction to food, alcohol, or drugs; obsessive/compulsive behavior, such as compulsive shopping, shoplifting, gambling, or cleaning; eating disorders; flashbacks triggered by certain sights, sounds, smells, or touches; abusive behavior toward others; self-destructive behavior, such as suicide attempts or self-mutilation.*

Physical Problems. *Frequent sore throats, difficulty swallowing, migraine headaches, unexplained vaginal or anal pain, frequent bladder and vaginal infections, skin disorders, numbness or tingling in legs or arms.*

MYTH #3

The abuser in childhood sexual abuse is always male.

Although most sexual offenses against children *are* perpetrated by males, many children are molested by females. In fact, as more and more reports of child sexual abuse are made, we are discovering that there are more female perpetrators than we ever imagined. Children have been sexually abused by their mothers, grandmothers, aunts, older sisters, older cousins, baby-sitters, older girls in the neighborhood, and female teachers and coaches.

The most common type of childhood sexual abuse perpetrated by females is that of mothers molesting their small children. These mothers, especially the ones who molest their infants and toddlers, are often emotionally disturbed or even psychotic and are often reenacting the sexual abuse that they experienced as children. Mothers have been known to fondle or suck a child's genitals, insert objects into the child's vagina or anus, or force the child to fondle or suck their breasts or genitals. Many of these mothers project their shame onto their daughters, seeing them as bad and dirty. Viewing their daughter's genitals as dirty, they may scrub them until they are raw. These same mothers often give frequent, unnecessary enemas to both their male and female children.

Some mothers, emotionally isolated as children and incapable of expressing affection appropriately, see their children (especially their daughters) as extensions of themselves. They may stimulate their children sexually in order to satisfy their own needs for pleasure, or they may actually believe that their actions are demonstrations of affection.

With their male children, mothers who were themselves sexually abused may be reenacting their abuse, this time as the ones who have the power. Molesting their sons may be the only time they feel powerful over males. Mother/son incest is probably the most subtly traumatic of all forms of incest. Since the incestuous mother cannot easily force her son, she must use seductiveness. This seductiveness turns out to be deadly, since the boy cannot help but respond and then feels horribly guilty afterward. The long-term effects of this kind of abuse range from impotency to self-destructiveness. The victim, usually resentful of women, often becomes a child molester, a rapist, or even a murderer.

Both male and female children are often molested by their young female baby-sitters. These girls, themselves victims of childhood sexual abuse, are also repeating the pattern of abuse and taking advantage of the fact that they have power over someone weaker than themselves. A good number of males who were sexually abused by female baby-sitters don't consider the occurrence to have been sexual abuse. When asked whether they were ever sexually abused, many of my male clients will tell me they were not. But when they are asked to describe their first sexual experiences, they often reveal that they were introduced to sex by a female baby-sitter when they were as young as two, three, or four years old. Because they sometimes remember feeling physically aroused by the experience, they consider it to have been a good thing, something that gave them a sort of "head start" on sex. They don't understand the damage done by their having become sexualized at such an early age and by the betrayal of trust involved.

Female baby-sitters or older neighborhood girls may also introduce girls much younger than themselves to sex. These experiences may be more traumatic, since it may cause the child to doubt her sexuality and since girls are taught to feel more guilt-ridden about sex than boys are. A child in this situation is more likely to feel ashamed and guilty, tending to blame herself for having allowed it to happen.

While sexual abuse of younger children by older sisters is less frequent than by older brothers, it nevertheless does occur. It is important to remember than even though an older female would have difficulty forcing a younger male to have intercourse with her, she may be so seductive that the younger male cannot control his urges. Some older sisters *have* used force, holding their captives down while they fondle them, perform oral sex on them, or insert objects into the anus.

MYTH #4

Incest between a brother and a sister is more of a mutual encounter and is not sexual abuse.

To the contrary, incest between siblings *is* usually sexual abuse, since it most often occurs when an older sibling coerces, threatens, or forces a younger sibling into sexual acts that the younger child is ill equipped to handle. A sibling who is only two or three years older is both physically and emotionally stronger than the younger one, and thus there is an inequity of power. This gives the older sibling just enough of an edge to be able to overpower the younger sibling both physically and emotionally.

Even a one-year age difference between siblings can have enormous power implications for both parties. For example, an older brother may frequently be left in charge of his younger sister, and females in most families are taught to concede to males. In addition, males are physically stronger, and their superior strength can be physically intimidating to a younger sister, especially if the brother tends to be a bully. The sister goes along with what her brother wants out of fear or out of a need to gain his approval.

Sexual abuse also occurs between same-sex siblings, though not as frequently as other types of sibling abuse. Again, this should not be confused with sex play or exploration among same-age peers.

In many cases, older siblings are reenacting the sexual abuse that they themselves have experienced. Having been traumatized and overpowered by someone stronger, they are now acting out their anger and pain by abusing someone less powerful than they are. Many a child molester's first victim was a younger sibling. Older siblings who have been violated themselves are often capable of being extremely violent toward younger siblings, threatening them or forcefully raping or sodomizing them.

In general, the greater the age difference, the greater the betrayal of trust and the more violent the incest tends to be since a much older sibling has so much more physical power. In some cases of older brother/younger sister abuse, there is tremendous violence, with the brother using immense force.

When a brother or sister is five years or more older than the younger sibling, the younger child may see the older one as a parental figure. Thus, the sense of betrayal can be almost as great as that experienced by a child whose parent betrays her trust.

Only under the following specific circumstances is sibling incest *not* sexual abuse:

---

1. *The children are young and are approximately the same age.*

2. *They have equal power, both with each other and in the family.*

3. *There is no coercion or physical force.*

4. *The sexual play is the result of natural curiosity, exploration, and mutual sexual naïveté.*

5. *The children are not traumatized by disapproving parents who may "catch them in the act."*

MYTH #5

Far more girls are sexually abused than boys, and even when a boy is molested it doesn't affect him that much.

As mentioned in the preface, the latest figures indicate that one in three children have been sexually abused. Because males tend to be even more reluctant to report experiences of child sexual abuse than females, the numbers may actually be higher than reported.

Males in our culture are traditionally supposed to be dominant, aggressive, and confident, with females submissive and passive. Males are supposed to be the seducers and controllers, while females are supposed to be the ones who are seduced or coerced into having sex. These very distinctions between what we expect of males and females add to the difficulties facing male survivors of sexual abuse.

Since women are already seen as passive beings, society more easily sympathizes with them when they are victimized. We have far more difficulty empathizing with male victims. Males are supposed to be able to protect themselves (and others), and if they are unable to do so, they are seen as weak. A male victim is usually perceived as being something less than a man, regardless of the situation.

When a boy is sexually abused, he is in essence revictimized by his culture and by his own tendency to be critical of himself. He likely views himself as a coward for "allowing it to happen" in the first place and for not avenging the crime. Even at a very young age, he considers himself weak for his inability to forget the experience and to simply "tough out" the emotional fallout.

Whether the perpetrator of the abuse was a male or a female, most male victims (as is true of many female victims) assume they must have done something to encourage the advances. Because most abusers are male, many male victims come to question their sexual orientation when they reach adolescence, even if the abuse occurred years earlier. They assume they must be homosexual for a man to have approached them to begin with. Randy, an adult heterosexual survivor who was molested by an older boy in the neighborhood when he was nine years old, recently told me:

"I was always afraid that I must be gay, because otherwise why would this guy pick on me? To make matters worse, I got an erection when he touched me, and it felt good. That really made me sure I must be gay. But I've since discovered that it feels good to have *anyone* touch my penis. It didn't mean I was gay because my body responded to touch the way it should."

Boys who were already aware of being attracted to other males, on the other hand, often reach adulthood convinced that the sexual attack was their deserved punishment for having had homoerotic thoughts. At 35, Mark is just beginning to accept his homosexuality.

"I always blamed myself for being sexually abused because I had an adolescent crush on the man who molested me. He was my high school wrestling coach, and I had fantasies about him all the time. When he started paying special attention to me, I was flattered. One day he asked me to help him out after school with some gym equipment, and he raped me—violently—in the equipment room. Years afterward, I felt like I must have deserved rape for being attracted to a man. This incident made me hate myself for any homosexual feelings I had from that time on."

Some male survivors feel unable to define themselves as sexual beings at all, because for them sexuality has become associated with abuse. Terence's case is a good example:

"My stepmother began to seduce me from the time she moved into our house when I was 13. She would walk around the house with hardly anything on, and she'd 'accidentally' walk in on me when I was in the bathroom. She was always having me rub her back, supposedly because it was sore. This behavior went on all during high school, when I should have been dating girls. I felt both turned on and repulsed by her, and this is how I still feel about women in general, 15 years later. I can become attracted to them, but if they become the slightest bit aggressive with me, I lose all interest. I feel so ashamed about the feelings I had for my stepmother that I just can't seem to develop any confidence with a woman."

In our society, sexual activity between women and boys is rarely treated as abusive. In fact, it is often glorified in movies and literature. A boy who comes forward and talks about having been sexually abused by a woman is often greeted by police, doctors, media, therapists, and even his family with disbelief or denial. They may trivialize or even romanticize his story. Faced with this situation, the boy may redefine his experiences to fit in with other people's perceptions, even to the point of bragging or joking about the incident(s).

In addition to the low self-esteem and feelings of inferiority suffered by all victims of sexual abuse, many male victims tend to feel less masculine than other males or, worse, less human. Feeling branded and irreparably damaged, they believe that no female would now want them. To counteract these feelings, many victims go to great lengths to prove their masculinity. They become sexually promiscuous, sexually violent, or overly controlling of women, or they attack other men they view as weaker than themselves. Some become daredevils, risking their lives to prove their manhood.

Because males are so embarrassed at having been sexually victimized, they cannot tolerate the feelings of helplessness that all victims feel. They short-circuit these feelings so that instead of identifying with other victims, they identify with those who seem powerful—the abusers. This is the beginning of the vicious circle in which sexually abused boys become sexually abusing men. (Women are more likely to repeat the cycle of abuse by continuing to be victimized.)

If the perpetrator of the sexual attack was a male and a primary role model, a male victim may well conclude that "being a man" means being abusive. He may believe, too, that he needs to inflict pain on another person before that person has a chance to inflict it on him. He may further conclude that the only way to empower himself is to make someone else a victim. As a result, many males who were sexually abused as children become child molesters, which of course adds to the shame they already feel and further discourages them from seeking professional help.

Adult males suffer from a variety of sexual problems as a direct result of childhood sexual abuse. The most common are an inability to achieve or maintain an erection, premature ejaculation or inability to ejaculate, fears of specific sexual acts (often those performed by the abuser or acts that the victim was forced to perform on the abuser), and painful intercourse. In addition, many male survivors suffer from sexual obsessions and fetishes, addiction to sex, compulsive masturbation, and a tendency to associate sex with humiliation and pain (which is often the case with individuals who practice sadomasochism).

MYTH #6

Most child molesters are strangers.

Many people still assume that most child molesters are strangers. This couldn't be further from the truth. While there are, indeed, pedophiles who lurk around schoolyards or other places frequented by children, the majority of perpetrators are relatives, most notably fathers, stepfathers, uncles, grandfathers, and older siblings, as well as mothers, grandmothers, and aunts. It has been estimated than 90 percent of child sexual abuse occurs in the home or at the hands of someone known to the family.

In his book *Child Sexual Abuse: New Theory and Research*, David Finkelhor notes that having a stepfather constitutes one of the strongest risk factors, more than doubling a girl's chance of being sexually molested. His study revealed that a stepfather is five times more likely than a natural father to sexually victimize a daughter.

Many children are sexually abused by coaches, camp counselors, baby-sitters, doctors, dentists, and so on—people the child trusts and/or cares about.

MYTH #7

A man who sexually abuses his child does so because he is not getting his sexual and emotional needs met by his wife.

Childhood sexual abuse, like rape, is an act of violence—an expression of anger and an exertion of power. It often has little or nothing to do with sexuality. Perpetrators abuse children in order to satisfy their own emotional needs—for example, the need to exercise power over someone, to seek revenge against a wife or mother for neglectful or abusive treatment, or to obtain something from the child that the perpetrator himself lacks desperately (such as love, innocence, or approval). Many child molesters are, in fact, unable to maintain a sexual relationship with an adult woman because of their overriding feelings of inadequacy and insecurity.

Some other perpetrators are sex addicts who use sex as a means of distracting themselves from their problems, "stuffing" their emotions, or temporarily building up their low self-esteem. Some perpetrators have been known to have sex with their wives two, three, or even four times a day, in addition to molesting children.

My client Georgia, the wife of a perpetrator, was shocked to discover that her husband was not only molesting their two daughters but was also having an affair with a neighbor woman.

"When I first realized that my husband was molesting our daughters, I blamed myself. He'd always complained to me that I didn't give him enough sex, even though he'd often demand it from me two or three times a day. I thought he had turned to the girls because he wasn't getting his needs met. But when I found out that he was also having sex regularly with another woman, I thought to myself, How often does he need sex, anyway? Since that time I have come to realize that my husband is addicted to sex, and that no matter how often I had sex with him it would never have been enough."

MYTH #8

A father who "loses control" and molests his daughter is not as bad as the child molester who goes around stalking children.

Many experts believe that the incestuous father is often just a child molester who stays home. Father/daughter incest is considered by many experts to be the most traumatic form of incestuous abuse because it damages the girl's relationship with men, severely damages her sexual self-esteem, and is a betrayal of trust.

There is general agreement that the roots of all incestuous assault are to be found in feelings of anger, insecurity, and isolation harbored by the aggressor. A father who molests his daughter may blame it on the victim or on his wife, on stress at work, on his alcoholism, on his unemployment, or on a myriad of other "causes." The truth is that the problem resides in the man himself. It is a result of his own childhood experiences, and it will travel with him wherever he goes. If you were to put him in another family and another situation, he would still molest a child. In this sense, he is no different from any other child molester.

Many people believe that a man may lose control with one of his children and molest her or him but never molest another child. The sad truth is that many incestuous fathers molest not only their own children, but also any other child who is accessible to them. Many of my female clients have been convinced that only they were molested, only to find out that their fathers molested the other daughters, too, and sometimes the sons as well. Other clients are even more hurt and shocked to discover that their fathers also molested their cousins, neighborhood children, or even the clients' own children.

MYTH #9

Just because a person makes a mistake and molests one child doesn't mean he will do it again with other children.

Rare is the perpetrator who molests once and then stops. Like an addict, he quickly becomes hooked. If anything, the molester's sexual activity accelerates after the first incident. The attempts often become more brash, the abuses occur more frequently, and the acts become more intrusive. The compulsion to repeat the sexual abuse is so great that the behavior is likely to continue even after he has been caught. Child molesters go to great lengths and put a vast amount of energy, time, and effort into maintaining their behavior, much like any addict. Many seek jobs, hobbies, and volunteer activities that involve youngsters. The incestuous stepfather who molests his stepchildren is likely to have abused other children outside the relationship, and he may even have married his wife because she had children.

While you may be shocked by what you have just read, it is essential that you know these things so that both you and the survivor can rid yourselves of any denial about childhood sexual abuse.

BELIEVE WHAT THE SURVIVOR TELLS YOU

Survivors need to know that the people closest to them believe them and are on their side. One of the most damaging events that can occur to a survivor is to have others refuse to believe them. Many survivors were not believed when they tried to get help as children, and many are still not believed by their families of origin today. You must recognize that the survivor is not lying or exaggerating. If anything, survivors of childhood sexual abuse tend to minimize what happened, how much it hurt them, and how terrible they feel about it.

Survivors need you to believe them for several reasons. First of all, as children enduring such abuse, they may have assumed that no one would believe them if they told, so they held in the secret—for months, years, even decades. Because they kept the secret for so long, they began to doubt their own perceptions and memories. As they enter therapy or begin a recovery program, they are encouraged to trust their perceptions and their recollections of the past. One word of disbelief from someone they care about, however, can throw them right back into self-doubt.

Again, the more you learn about the subject of child sexual abuse, the more you will realize that even though the things your partner or friend is telling you are hard for you to believe, such things do, indeed, occur.

ALLOW THE SURVIVOR THE TIME AND SPACE TO RELEASE HER ANGER

Survivors are, understandably, extremely angry people. Anyone who has been victimized and has not been through a recovery process is seething with anger at having been violated. Survivors of sexual abuse were usually unable to express their anger when they were children, because they were either afraid of the perpetrator or unable to fully grasp the fact that someone they trusted could do this to them.

Because survivors most often bury their feelings about the abuse or deny or minimize what happened, their anger becomes hidden so deeply inside that they are unaware of it until they begin working on their sexual abuse issues. Since the anger has been building up for so long, it often comes out explosively. It may bombard anyone and everyone in the survivor's path, or it may be focused primarily on the perpetrator or on a parent who was a silent partner in the abuse.

As I've stressed earlier, it is necessary for the survivor to express her anger, even if it seems inappropriate or extreme to you. You may become frightened that the survivor is going to get in trouble with her anger because it seems to burst out at the most inopportune times or in the form of constant conflicts with others. Trena shared with other members of her group her worries about her lover, Joanne:

"When Joanne first remembered that she had been molested by her stepfather, she started getting angry at men in general. If a guy just looked at her in a flirtatious way she became enraged. I remember one time this biker guy made some remark to us as we walked past him, and Joanne yelled at him to keep his dirty mouth shut. He called her a bitch, and Joanne went wild. She started yelling obscenities at him at the top of her lungs. Now this guy was a tough-looking character, and I was scared to death about what he was going to do, but I guess Joanne's anger must have scared even him. He just looked at her like she was weird and walked away. She got away with it that time, but I'm constantly afraid that she's going to blow up at the wrong person and get herself hurt."

Even though you may be afraid for the survivor, there is little you can do to protect her from her own emotions. Nine times out of ten, survivors do get through the anger phase without endangering themselves or others. They may bristle a lot and blow off a lot of steam, and they will undoubtedly be hard to get along with at times, but in general their anger is harmless. If the survivor is in therapy and/or in a support, recovery, or Twelve-Step group, the therapist or fellow group members will encourage her to find constructive ways of releasing anger. If the survivor is *not* in therapy or in a group, and you are concerned about the way she is handling anger, you may want to encourage her to seek outside help. Beyond doing this, all you can do is remind yourself that this phase will eventually pass. The best way for you to help is to give the survivor the understanding, space, and time to continue releasing her pent-up anger.

If the survivor focuses her anger on you, it will obviously become very uncomfortable for you. However, try not to take it personally. Keep in mind that she is just feeling so much anger that it is bound to spill over into her present-day life. If the survivor becomes abusive in any way, however—whether verbally, emotionally, physically, or sexually—you will need to make sure she stops.

If you were raised in an environment where there was a lot of chaos, fighting, or verbal or physical abuse, you may find yourself propelled back into your childhood when the survivor displays her anger. You may become frightened or enraged, and you may experience such physical reactions as numbness, shakiness, nausea or tightness of the stomach, tension in your jaw or shoulders, or clenching of your fists. These are all signs that you are reacting not just to the survivor's anger but to some event, circumstance, or person in your life, most likely from your childhood.

If you come from a home where there was verbal or physical abuse you will have a very low tolerance for the expression of anger. Take care of yourself by not being around the survivor when she is expressing her anger about the abuse. At the same time, take responsibility for the fact that these are *your* reactions, based on your own personal experience, and don't make the survivor feel responsible and guilty for the fact that you feel these feelings.

Perhaps you were not allowed to express your anger when you were a child, or perhaps you were taught that anger is a weakness or even a sin. However, the expression of anger is necessary and healthy; in fact, it has been found that the repression of anger can cause all kinds of problems, from depression to such physical ailments as ulcers and high blood pressure. While you have a right to your own beliefs about anger, you do not have the right to impose those beliefs on the survivor, who is in the process of learning that anger is a healthy emotion and that she needs to find constructive ways to release it. If you tell her the opposite, either directly or indirectly, you will be hindering her recovery.

ALLOW THE SURVIVOR TO PLACE THE BLAME WHERE IT BELONGS

Most survivors blame themselves for the abuse. No matter how often they are told that the abuse was not their fault, that they didn't ask for it, and that they were innocent, they don't really believe it. They may understand it intellectually, but they don't believe it emotionally. For this reason, therapists encourage survivors to begin to place the blame where it belongs—on the perpetrator.

Although we all blame others, it is not something that is encouraged in our society. In fact, we are constantly being told that we should not blame others. Religious leaders, talk-show therapists, and self-help books may tell us that blaming is unhealthy for us and those we blame. While there is much to be said for this point of view and for forgiveness in general, survivors of sexual abuse need to be able to blame their perpetrators for a time to offset the burden of blame they impose on themselves.

Many people believe that survivors need to work toward forgiving the perpetrator and silent partners. However, the issue of forgiveness is something every survivor must decide for herself or himself. Forgiveness is difficult and sometimes impossible. There are many, many people who, no matter how hard they try, have been unable to forgive those who abused or neglected them when they were children. *It is not necessary for a survivor to forgive in order to recover or to go on with her life.*

If the abuser is willing to accept responsibility for his actions and to apologize to the survivor, she may feel like forgiving him. But if the abuser refuses to admit that he caused damage and to apologize for that damage, the survivor may not feel that forgiveness is in order. In fact, some survivors have deliberately chosen *not* to forgive as a way of maintaining a needed distance from the person who abused them and as a way of guaranteeing that they will not be manipulated into a situation where they will be abused again.

Many survivors actually have a harder time withholding forgiveness than they do in forgiving. They have a tendency to forgive too quickly, often failing to consider their own needs. In an attempt to please their parents or others who say that they should forgive, they may push down their anger—anger that can actually help them to recover—in an effort to "forgive." Ironically, it is only after we have been able to release our anger that we are truly able to forgive.

If during the process of recovery the survivor gets to the place where she can forgive, she will undoubtedly feel a sense of relief and freedom from the past. But it is important for both of you to recognize that forgiving doesn't mean forgetting or ignoring the past. What it means is that the survivor no longer carries the anger from the past with her today.

ALLOW THE SURVIVOR THE TIME AND SPACE TO FEEL HER PAIN

Survivors need plenty of time and space to cry all the tears they were never allowed to shed, to feel the pain of the betrayal and the intrusion of sexual abuse. They need to mourn the loss of their innocence, their childhood, their trust, and their self-esteem.

Once again, as with overt displays of anger, your own upbringing may influence how you react to the survivor's pain and crying. If you were scolded for crying, told that big kids (or boys) don't cry, or even punished for crying, you may have internalized these injunctions and now be passing them on to others. While your parents may have had good intentions in discouraging you from crying, we have learned that crying is an extremely necessary act, one that promotes healing of both physical and emotional wounds.

Survivors gain strength by crying. They are not displaying weakness. They are getting healthier with each tear they shed. And don't worry, they won't cry forever—just long enough to heal their wounds.

RESPECT THE TIME AND SPACE IT TAKES TO HEAL

The recovery process is long and slow. Pressure from you as to why it is taking so long will only prolong the recovery time. Survivors may already feel that there is something terribly wrong with them because they can't seem to "get over it" and get on with their lives; complaints that they aren't recovering fast enough may further damage their already low self-esteem.

It is natural for you to become impatient at times, especially since you may not see any obvious improvement in your partner or friend for quite some time. But as noted earlier, it can take up to five years or even longer for a survivor to recover from such a devastating trauma. Sometimes the changes she makes will be very evident, and at other times they will not be. Just because you don't see the kinds of visible changes that you had hoped for doesn't mean that the survivor is not recovering.

It is also natural for you to feel threatened by the amount of time that the survivor spends at her therapy sessions or group meetings, particularly if it takes away from time she would ordinarily spend with you. The same holds true of the amount of time she spends with other survivors. This might be a good time for you to join a prosurvivors' group, or to make some new friends. And try to remember that the survivor will probably end up being a better friend, lover, spouse, or parent to your children after she completes the recovery process.

Because the survivor cares about you, she cares about your opinion. Survivors tend to be easily influenced by others, so be aware that any complaints you make about her therapy, her therapist, the length of time her recovery is taking, or the amount of money it is costing can cause the survivor to doubt herself, her therapist, and the recovery process. Survivors already have a difficult enough time learning to trust others; don't reinforce this tendency by casting doubts on what her therapist is doing. Trust that she is the best judge of whether she is getting the kind of help she needs.

Often, survivors are encouraged by their therapists and by members of a recovery group to do things that may seem bizarre to you (for example, carrying around a stuffed animal, talking out loud to an imaginary perpetrator, or coloring with crayons). Try to realize that there is a good reason for having survivors do these kinds of things, and trust that your partner or friend is getting some benefit from them.

If the survivor tends to constantly complain about her therapist or recovery group, don't automatically agree with her or suggest that she quit. Instead, suggest that she share her feelings with her therapist or with the members of her group. Survivors need to be encouraged to express their feelings directly to the people they are upset with so they can learn that it is safe to do so. It is common for survivors to experience feelings of resistance during the recovery process, and they need to talk these feelings out with their therapist or group so they can learn to differentiate resistance from legitimate complaints.

The only time when it would be appropriate for you to interfere with a survivor's therapy would be if you believed that she was being further victimized by an unscrupulous therapist. Unfortunately, there are therapists who use their roles as authority figures to take advantage of their clients sexually, and in other ways. Some therapists have been known to have sex with their clients in their office and to actually charge them for a visit, asserting that having sex with the therapist is necessary in order for the client to overcome sexual problems or fears of intimacy.

If the survivor tells you, or if you suspect, that her therapist is becoming sexual with her in any way, let her know that she is being reabused, that what the therapist is doing is illegal, and that she needs to find another therapist. Furthermore, suggest that she tell her next therapist about the situation she experienced with the previous therapist, since she will need help to overcome this most recent abuse, and the new therapist can help her decide whether she wants to take legal action against the abusive therapist. While there certainly are incompetent therapists, unless you suspect an obvious breach in ethics such as the therapist becoming sexually involved with your friend or lover, you need to stay out of it and trust that she or he will take care of herself. If your friend or lover tells you of other practices that seem to be unethical, by all means encourage her to find another therapist.

UNDERSTAND THAT YOU MUST EARN THE SURVIVOR'S TRUST

As noted, childhood sexual abuse destroys the survivor's ability to trust. From earliest childhood we are warned that *strangers* are dangerous, but seldom, if ever, are we told that family members, friends of the family, doctors, teachers, and so on can also be dangerous. While a child who has been attacked by a stranger can retreat to the safety of home, to be comforted by Mommy and Daddy, where is the refuge and comfort for the child who has been abused *by* Mommy or Daddy?

When your first sexual experience is abuse, you learn some terrible things about people and about life. You learn that people will do almost anything in order to satisfy their own selfish needs. You learn that someone can tell you he loves you one minute and hurt you deeply the next. You learn that when someone says he is asking for something out of love, it may instead be out of lust and selfishness.

Survivors tend to feel that a partner's thoughts and intentions are similar to those of the perpetrator. The survivor may not believe you when you tell her that you love her, because it may have been this same assertion that allowed the perpetrator to do what he wanted. She might believe that you, like the perpetrator, are only out to satisfy your own sexual needs but do not really care about her emotional welfare.

Your partner or friend must learn through experience with you that she can trust you—trust that you love her, that you will not betray her, and that you are not going to use her like the perpetrator did. Ever so slowly, she must learn that you are different from the perpetrator, that she can indeed trust someone again. *This will take time*—she cannot just will herself to trust.

It may not feel good to you to have to prove yourself to someone. After all, none of us like to be in this position. We assume that others should know that we are trustworthy, and it offends us when they do not. I remember feeling this way when I first began to work with survivors and was faced with their constant distrust of me. But I soon began to understand that they really had no reason to trust me—after all, they didn't really know me. While I felt that I was trustworthy, they had no way of knowing this to be true, and my word alone was certainly not sufficient. I began to realize that I was going to have to earn their trust, a little bit at a time. Now I feel so strongly about it that I sometimes tell new clients that they should *not* trust me until I have earned their trust!

No one, of course, is completely, 100 percent trustworthy. We all have our weaknesses and faults, and you are no exception. You would be doing your partner a great disservice if you told her that she could trust you completely at all times. The most truly loving approach would be to tell her the truth about yourself, letting her know the ways in which she can and cannot trust you. For example, she may be able to trust you to keep your word and to be faithful to her, but she may not be able to trust that you won't sometimes deliberately hurt her if your feelings are hurt. The point here is not that you want to be excused for bad or untrustworthy behavior, but that it is important to be realistic and to acknowledge that despite our best intentions, we can't promise perfection.

Being honest with the survivor about who you are and what she can expect from you is one of the best things you can do for her. Many people don't know themselves well enough to share these things with their partners, even if they are willing to do so. Start by thinking about the things you value most in yourself. Now think about the characteristics you do not like about yourself, the ones that continually get you into trouble. Take some time to think about how you have been in past relationships, remembering especially the complaints other partners have had about you. It might help your self-evaluation process to ask yourself the following questions:

---

1. *If you say you are going to do something, do you generally do it?*

2. *Do you keep your promises?*

3. *Do you usually keep your dates and appointments?*

4. *Do you usually arrive when you say you will?*

5. *Do you lie in order to get what you want?*

6. *Do you reveal secrets even though you have promised not to?*

7. *Do you sometimes stretch the truth or exaggerate in order to make yourself look better?*

8. *Do you sometimes say things you don't mean or falsely flatter people in order to get something out of them?*

9. *Have you ever been unfaithful to a partner?*

If you answered yes to most of items 1–4 and no to most of items 5–9, you are an exceptionally trustworthy person. On the other hand, if you answered no to most of items 1–4 and yes to most of items 5–9, you are exceptionally *un*trustworthy. Most people fall somewhere in between. We've all broken promises and let people down. All of us lie, all of us exaggerate, and all of us manipulate. The real sin here would be to portray yourself as a saint to your partner and to then continually let her down. She doesn't deserve to be betrayed, manipulated, or disappointed one more time. Letting her know your degree of trustworthiness and being honest about it can be a real gift to her.

The best way to build trust, of course, will be for you to prove to your partner or friend that she can rely on you, that you will keep your word. If you say you are going to do something, by all means make every effort to do so. Otherwise, don't promise to do it. If you tell her that you just want to give her a massage and that you will not try to seduce her into sex, don't become sexual with her. Don't offer the massage as a way of manipulating her into letting you touch her sexually or in an attempt to arouse her.

DON'T TRY TO RESCUE THE SURVIVOR

Try to see your partner or friend not as a weak victim but as the strong, courageous survivor that she is. While she needs your support and understanding, she does not need you to take care of her, take away her bad feelings, or tell her what to do. She has probably had enough people in her life who have tried to control her and direct her life for her. Now she needs to become more independent and to trust her own ability to take care of herself.

While she may at times try to get you to take care of her (as she probably has in the past), try not to get hooked into it. She'll need time to make the change from being a dependent, insecure person who doesn't trust her own judgment and abilities to being the independent, self-assured person she can become.

The suggestions made in this chapter will help you to implement some changes immediately in how you treat the survivor in your life. Now that you know what she needs from you, you can apply it to the various stages of recovery. The next chapter will outline these stages and will offer you specific ways to support the survivor during each stage of recovery.

Chapter Three

What to Expect:

Phases in Recovery

During the course of recovery, survivors of childhood sexual abuse go through several different stages necessary for their healing. While it is important to remember that each survivor is a unique person with his or her own particular life experiences, most survivors go through certain predictable phases. Not all go through each stage at the same point in recovery or in the same order in which they are discussed here.

STAGE ONE: FACING THE TRUTH

In the first phase, survivors begin to face the fact that they were sexually abused. They may not have specific memories yet, but only a vague inner "knowing" or a strong suspicion. They may recognize that they exhibit many of the symptoms of survivors of childhood sexual abuse. They may have been told that someone else in their family was sexually abused and fear that the perpetrator may have abused them also, or they may have flashes of memory or nightmares that indicate sexual abuse. They may recently have begun to notice sexual problems; suffer unexplained pain in their vagina, penis, or anus; wake up at the same time every night; or be afraid to go to sleep.

Acknowledgment is the first major sign of recovery, for it is only when a survivor acknowledges having been abused that he or she can begin to heal. Unfortunately, facing the fact that one was sexually abused as a child is a painful and difficult step. Typically, survivors will go in and out of denial. One moment they're convinced that they were, indeed, abused, only to change their mind the next moment, or perhaps hours or days later. They will constantly doubt their own perceptions and memories, fluctuating between believing these and thinking that they are making it all up.

During this phase, survivors will be focused on bringing forth memories to validate their suspicions, perhaps by going back into their past and trying to remember their childhood through old photographs, returning to houses they used to live in, or by talking to family members. Those who are working with an individual therapist may be assisted in this through hypnosis or other regression techniques.

If the perpetrator was a family member or someone the survivor loved or was especially close to, admitting the abuse will be particularly difficult. This is especially true when the perpetrator was a parent. The child is then torn between feelings of love, loyalty, and dependence and feelings of anger, fear, and betrayal.

During this time of remembering, survivors will also have to face the truth about their family of origin. Sometimes this will mean acknowledging that their parent or parents, siblings, or grandparents did not protect them, did not believe them when they tried to tell what had happened, allowed the abuse to occur or even participated in it, and perhaps set them up for the abuse by bringing an abusive, emotionally unstable, or alcoholic person into their lives.

Needless to say, this will be a very difficult time for survivors as they face what they have tried all their lives to forget. If they are able to remember the abuse itself, they will feel retraumatized by their memories and will be facing feelings that they may not have been capable of feeling at the time. Feelings of pain, fear, shame, guilt, and anger will surface as they once again experience the devastation of being violated and of feeling utterly alone with their pain and fear.

Many will go through a period of mourning as they give up the fantasy that they had a "normal" childhood and that their parents loved and protected them. They will also have to mourn the loss of their innocence and their childhood. All during this first phase the survivor will experience periods of moodiness, crying spells, and depression.

The best way for you to support your partner or friend during this first stage is to allow her to face the truth in her own time, without pressuring her or trying to influence her in any way. For example, while you may have come to the conclusion that she was, indeed, sexually abused by her father, it is not your place to try to convince her that it is true. She may have in fact told you that this did happen, only to "forget" that she told you, or to change her mind and take it all back. Recognize that she may need to go in and out of denial for some time before she can finally admit the truth to herself or to anyone else. Don't try to push her into facing anything she is not yet prepared to face.

When she is able to admit the truth to herself, she may move into another phase of needing to tell others. It may seem to you that she has to tell *everyone*, and this may embarrass you. Or, she may need to tell you her story again and again, until you feel tired of hearing it. Try to be patient, and to realize that it is the telling of her story that makes the experience real for her. Each time she tells it, she is able to feel more of the emotions attached to the experience.

As mentioned earlier, it is vitally important that you believe the survivor when she discloses the abuse to you. Even if some or all of what she is saying sounds improbable to you, there is truth to everything she is saying. While parts of her story may still be missing, while she may not yet be able to clearly identify who the perpetrator was or what the circumstances were, believe her when she tells you she was abused. She will be able to fill in the details as she progresses further in her recovery.

When the survivor was being sexually abused, those around her acted as if it wasn't happening. Since no one else acknowledged the abuse, she sometimes felt that it wasn't real or that it must not have been a bad thing. Because the person who abused her did not acknowledge her pain, she may have thought that perhaps it wasn't as bad as she felt it was.

Unless they face the truth about their childhood, including the truth about those who abused them, survivors of childhood sexual abuse cannot fully recover. Part of facing the truth involves telling those close to them exactly what happened to them, without minimizing it or denying their feelings about it.

If in the process of telling the truth the survivor is questioned about the accuracy of her disclosure, she may go back into minimizing and denial. In the rare situation where the survivor can hold onto the truth in the face of disbelief from her lover or friend, the sense of betrayal she feels can damage and even destroy any trust that has been built up in the relationship.

STAGE TWO: RELEASING ANGER

Once the survivor has come out of denial and has begun to face the truth, she will inevitably become angry. While she will also continue to feel a tremendous amount of pain and to mourn all her losses during the entire recovery process, the emotion that will have the strongest impact on her recovery, and that will be her strongest ally, is anger. The more a survivor faces the truth, the more angry she will become. She has the right to feel angry at any and all of the following people:

- The perpetrator
- Her parents
- Other members of her family of origin who didn't protect her
- Anyone who made her vulnerable to the abuser
- Anyone who excused or protected the abuser
- Anyone who should have been concerned but didn't act
- Anyone who didn't believe her when she tried to tell
- Anyone who told her to forget it or told her it wasn't any big deal
- Anyone who blamed her
- Anyone who told her that she wanted it or that she did it for her own pleasure

Most survivors seem to start by focusing their anger on the parent who did not protect them, the silent partner. This is partly because they may still feel intimidated by the perpetrator, but it is also because survivors often feel just as betrayed by the nonprotective parent. They may focus their anger on the nonprotective parent for months or even years, especially if this parent continues to protect the perpetrator or refuses to believe the abuse occurred.

Eventually, the survivor will need to focus her anger on the perpetrator in order to complete her recovery. This is a very difficult phase for most survivors, for several reasons: the very person who abused them may have been the only one who paid them any attention, they may still be afraid of the abuser, and they may still blame themselves for the abuse. By the time survivors have worked past these roadblocks to their free expression of anger, they are well on the road to recovery.

As noted earlier, the survivor may ventilate her anger at anyone and everyone she has dealings with, especially those closest to her. This may mean that she may begin to pick on you, finding fault in everything you do. She may fly into rages as her anger begins to build up. Or, she may continue to take her anger out on herself, becoming extremely depressed, self-destructive, or even suicidal.

The survivor needs to learn constructive ways of releasing her anger so that she will not hurt others or herself. If she is in individual therapy or in a support or recovery group, she will undoubtedly be taught these kinds of anger-releasing techniques. Don't be surprised if the survivor starts pounding the bed with a tennis racket or a foam or plastic bat, tearing up telephone books, putting her head in a pillow and screaming, or going out to the garage and stomping on aluminum cans. These and many other anger-releasing techniques are recommended to survivors as healthy, constructive ways of releasing pent-up anger.

The best support you can provide a survivor during Stage Two is to let her know that she has a right to her anger and to encourage her to find constructive ways of releasing it. As mentioned in the previous chapter, you will need to allow her the time and space to release her anger, and not try to talk her out of it or make her feel like a bad person for being angry.

STAGE THREE: CONFRONTING THE PERPETRATOR AND ANYONE ELSE WHO CONTRIBUTED TO THE DAMAGE

At some point in recovery—usually, after acknowledging that she truly was a victim and releasing some of her repressed anger—the survivor will need to confront those who damaged her: the perpetrator, the silent partner, and any other family member who either set her up for the abuse or did nothing to stop it. This confrontation can be either direct (meaning that you involve the person you are confronting) or indirect (meaning that you don't). Whether she chooses to confront directly or indirectly, the survivor will likely experience a tremendous amount of satisfaction when she stands up to those who hurt her and expresses her anger and pain.

Confronting is different from releasing anger in that its purpose is for survivors to stand up to those who hurt them in an assertive rather than an angry fashion. Survivors are encouraged to ventilate their anger *before* they confront so that they can communicate their feelings in a strong, clear, self-assured manner, instead of exploding and losing control.

They are also encouraged to rehearse their confrontation, or plan what they are going to say ahead of time, so they are able to say exactly what they want to say. Generally speaking, it is recommended that survivors include the following in their confrontation:

1. *Exactly what the person did to them that caused them damage.*

2. *What effect the person's actions (or inaction) had on them, and how their life has been affected.*

3. *What they would have wanted from the person at the time.*

4. *How they feel about the person now and what they want from them now.*

Many survivors are still too afraid of the perpetrator to confront him face-to-face and this may be wise, since some perpetrators are still so abusive that a survivor might be endangering herself if she were to confront the abuser in this way. On the other hand, where the situation is not dangerous, many survivors gain a tremendous sense of personal power by standing up to someone they have been afraid of all their lives. If a face-to-face confrontation is not possible or is too threatening, there are other ways that survivors can confront directly, such as writing and then mailing a letter, recording their thoughts and then sending or giving the tape to the person, or confronting on the telephone.

Still other survivors choose not to confront the perpetrator or family member directly. Indirect confrontation can be accomplished through role-playing (with the survivor having an imaginary conversation with the perpetrator) or through writing a letter or making a tape recording that is *not* sent to the other party.

In order to support your mate or friend during this stage, you will need to respect her enough to trust that she knows best just who, how, and when to confront. She does not need you to protect her or to do her confronting for her, nor does she need you to tell her how to go about it. Try to keep your judgments to yourself so that you don't influence her in this important decision.

Whatever method the survivor uses to confront those who have damaged her, the results will generally be the same. She will feel empowered, less like a victim, and less likely to allow anyone to abuse her again. She will feel proud of herself for having made the confrontation, and this pride will carry over into other aspects of her life, including her relationship with you. Having completed some of her "unfinished business" with those from her past, she may now feel more like dealing with issues that have been building up concerning her present relationships. She may choose this time to confront you about behavior she feels is abusive or unloving on your part, and she may begin to assert her needs and desires far more often than she ever did before.

STAGE FOUR: RESOLVING FAMILY RELATIONSHIPS

Survivors have two major tasks to accomplish in relation to the members of their family of origin: the resolution of intense feelings, and the establishment of new boundaries with old family members. Resolving the intense, leftover feelings from the abuse allows the survivor to move on to create better relationships. As mentioned earlier, feelings such as anger, fear, betrayal, and sadness need to come to the surface and be expressed in safe, supportive ways. Sometimes this can occur directly, when family members are willing to be involved in a supportive way. Most often though, because other family members are not available or supportive or because negative consequences might ensue for the survivor, it is more appropriate for it to occur indirectly in the ways I have noted or through therapy. This letting go of old feelings frees the survivor from the victim role she may have played in the family. Understanding and resolving feelings allows her to live a life unencumbered by continual bitterness and hatred.

After the survivor has confronted the perpetrator and/or members of her family of origin, either directly or indirectly, some kind of resolution is called for so that she can go on with her life. A survivor may choose to temporarily separate from or even "divorce" family members, or she may choose to reconcile with them. The choice is solely hers to make, and it should not be influenced by what you or anyone else thinks. She will make this decision by determining which relationships are healthy and which are not, by confronting family members and opening up the lines of communication, and by learning healthier, more assertive ways of communicating with them.

Many survivors decide on temporary separation from one or both parents and/or from other members of their childhood family while they are going through the recovery process. This gives them much-needed time to work on their issues without interference from their families, time to separate emotionally from their families and learn to stand on their own, and time to heal from their wounds and thus be better able to reassess their family relationships later on.

Often, survivors find that their progress is continually thwarted each time they see their parents. This is especially true if one or both parents are still in denial about the sexual abuse, or if they are especially controlling and domineering. When this is the case, the survivor may begin to doubt her perceptions and even to doubt that she was abused. Or, she may revert to being a subservient or fearful child who allows her parents to dictate how she should act. It is rare to find a family who rallies around the survivor, providing her with the support and understanding she so much needs. Instead, families often cause the survivor to feel guilty for bringing up the abuse in the first place, for not "forgiving and forgetting," and for causing trouble in the family. Instead of offering support, they often try to undermine the survivor's attempts at recovery by criticizing therapy in general or by finding fault with the survivor's therapist.

There is no prescribed or recommended amount of time for a

temporary separation from one's family members. Each survivor must decide this on her own. Some survivors stay away only a few months, while others count the time by years. Some break completely, having no contact whatsoever with their parents or families, while others limit the time they spend with them (sometimes keeping contact confined to important functions such as weddings, funerals, and important holidays). Others communicate only by mail or telephone.

How a survivor chooses to establish adult relationships with the offender and other family members is an individual decision, based on a variety of circumstances. The key is that the survivor needs to give herself permission to limit contact and possibly to change the entire nature of the contact, if that's what she requires in order to affirm her strength and separateness. Some survivors choose to reestablish contact or to reconcile with their parents or other family members only after they have gained assertiveness and self-protection skills, learned to reduce their expectations of how much closeness is possible, and lessened their need for love and support from their families of origin.

The decision to "divorce" her parents or other family members may be the only alternative when the relationship is so destructive that the survivor must choose between her health and her family. Being around family members who deny that the sexual abuse ever occurred, who accuse the survivor of lying or exaggerating, or who continue to protect the perpetrator, can be extremely damaging to the survivor and can get in the way of her recovery.

Permanent separation is usually the only healthy choice for a survivor if either or both parents do the following:

➤ If they continue to abuse her physically, sexually, or emotionally, and she has either not become able to stand up for herself or her attempts to stop the abuse haven't worked.

➤ If they continue to deny that she was sexually abused, persist in protecting the perpetrator, or blame her for the abuse.

➤ If they continue to make her doubt her perceptions, memory, or sanity.

- ➤ If they abuse the survivor's children or will not protect them from someone who is abusive.
- ➤ If they are emotionally disturbed, or are practicing alcoholics or drug addicts and refuse to get help.
- ➤ If the relationship is so destructive that it is a threat to the survivor's physical or emotional health.
- ➤ If having contact with one or both parents interferes with the survivor's recovery or her progress in therapy.

Naturally, if the survivor does choose to divorce herself from one or both parents, she will feel the burden of her pain and loss. Even those who haven't seen their parents in a long time have considerable difficulty when it comes to permanently severing the ties. If the survivor in your life is not already in therapy or in a support group, encourage her to do so before she attempts this momentous task, or encourage her to read my book, *Divorcing a Parent*.

If she decides to divorce one or both of her parents, or to sever all ties with other family members, she will need your support more than ever. It is a painful thing to say good-bye to your family, no matter how abusive or neglectful they have been. The survivor will need you to be her new family and to comfort her as she mourns her old one.

Some survivors are able to reconcile successfully with their parents and other family members, either because they have become strong enough to stand up for themselves or because the family has changed adequately.

The best way to support the survivor during Stage Four is to allow her to resolve her relationships with her family in the way that feels best to her, *not* in the way that you think she should. Although she may frequently be confused about what she should do and may vacillate between wanting contact with her parents and wanting nothing to do with them, don't get hooked into giving her advice. Let her struggle through this extremely important decision on her own.

STAGE FIVE: SELF-DISCOVERY

During this phase, the survivor will need to focus on discovering just who she is, separate from her family, from the perpetrator, and from you. Because the survivor had little, if any, opportunity during childhood and adolescence to develop her own identity or sense of self, she must do this now.

One of the best ways of discovering just who we are is to focus on what we feel at any given time. For many survivors, focusing on how they feel may seem extremely alien, since they are so used to avoiding and numbing their feelings.

The survivor will need a lot of time alone to increase her self-awareness and self-knowledge, and she will need a lot of permission to explore her emotions.

She may seem terribly preoccupied at this time, spending a great deal of time alone. As difficult as it might be for you, keep in mind that by far the best way you can support the survivor in her self-discovery process is to give her this time. Reassure her that you care and that you will be available if she needs to talk, then find ways of meeting your own needs. This might be an excellent time for you to take advantage of the opportunity to do some self-reflection of your own. You need to keep growing emotionally yourself so that when the survivor is able to refocus on the relationship, you will be as strong, independent, and self-aware as she will be.

STAGE SIX: LEARNING SELF-CARE

Learning to take care of themselves is not easy for survivors. Most either neglect themselves terribly, even to the point of being self-destructive, or focus too much of their time and energy on taking care of others. Survivors are often more comfortable being care-givers than care-receivers. They have difficulty asking for what they need and have difficulty receiving gifts or compliments.

During Stage Six, it will be important for the survivor to acknowledge how very important her own needs are. This can mean learning how to put her own needs first, to take better care of her body, and to respect her privacy and boundaries and insist that others do the same. It may mean learning how to give herself the nurturing, encouragement, and praise she never received as a child. She may need to learn to be more assertive, to ask for what she wants, to say no to what she doesn't want, and to recognize her choices and rights. Many survivors discover for the first time that they have a right to express their feelings, opinions, and needs and to make their own decisions.

Most survivors were never taught to take care of themselves in these ways. Instead, they were taught to take care of the perpetrator's or their parents' needs. Because they grew up hearing things like "Stop thinking of yourself all the time!" or "You're just a selfish brat!" they came to equate taking care of their own needs with selfishness. They also received nonverbal messages, such as "I can't meet your needs; I have too many of my own" or "I didn't get my needs met when I was a child, so you have to take care of me now."

You can support the survivor during this time by encouraging her to take care of her own needs first and to say no if she doesn't want to do something, and by not expecting her to take care of your needs quite so much. Although this will undoubtedly be difficult for you, remember that the better able the survivor is to take care of her own needs, the better chance you will have of establishing a healthy relationship.

STAGE SEVEN: SELF-FORGIVENESS

Survivors of childhood sexual abuse feel a tremendous amount of guilt and shame: for the abuse itself, for things they did as a child as a result of the abuse, and for things they have done as an adult to hurt themselves and others. These feelings of guilt and shame cause survivors to become self-destructive. They abuse their bodies with food, alcohol, drugs, cigarettes, and self-mutilation. They also become accident-prone, sabotage their success, and elicit punishment or mistreatment from others.

For this reason, self-forgiveness is one of the most important steps in the recovery process. Even though she may be told over and over by her therapist, members of her support group, or by you, that the sexual abuse was not her fault, and even if she knows this on a rational, intellectual level, deep down inside she probably still blames herself for her involvement in the abuse (for being submissive or passive, for not telling anyone, for her body's response).

The process of self-forgiveness will take a long time and actually occurs during the entire recovery process. Survivors must learn that they cannot be held responsible for so-called choices unless they are *free* choices. A free choice is made when we understand the consequences of our actions and are allowed to make a choice freely instead of being coerced, bribed, intimidated, or threatened into satisfying someone else's needs. Children and adolescents are too young to responsibly make a free choice to have sex with a perpetrator.

Another important aspect of self-forgiveness is learning to differentiate between what we are responsible for and what we are not. For example, as stated earlier, children are never responsible for any aspect of the sexual abuse itself. By the same token, a sexually abused child should not be held responsible for their behavior, no matter how abusive, since it was more than likely a reaction to the abuse they sustained. The issue becomes a little less clear-cut, however, when it comes to abusive behavior on an adolescent's part as a reaction to their own abuse. While adolescents are not typically held responsible for their behavior in the same way as adults, if your partner or friend sexually abused a younger child as a consequence of her own abuse, she does have some responsibility. She certainly is responsible for her behavior as an adult, whether it be stealing, abusing her children, or driving under the influence of alcohol or drugs. Even if her behavior was clearly a result of the sexual abuse, she is still accountable for it and she may need to make amends to those she has hurt before she can be relieved of her guilt. She may have to meet with those she has harmed, admit to them that what she did was wrong, apologize, and make restitution in the best way possible. For example, if she has stolen money, she will need to repay it, or if the person she hurt needs therapy as a result of her actions, she should offer to pay for it. These acts will help her begin to forgive herself for the harm she has done to others.

In order for survivors to recover, they must come to terms with both their innocence and their guilt. This means forgiving themselves for those things they had no responsibility for, holding themselves accountable for what they were responsible for, and making restitution for the harm they have done to others. While forgiving the abuser or their family is not always possible and is certainly not necessary for recovery, survivors do need to forgive themselves.

For both of you, understanding the recovery process and knowing what to expect will make the process easier. This doesn't, of course, mean that you both still won't go through some very difficult times; that is inevitable. It will be important to remember that *it does get easier*. The more the survivor recovers, the less tumultuous your lives will be, and the more she will be able to relate to you in ways that are fulfilling for both of you.

In Part I we have focused on how you can better understand and support the survivor. In Part II, we will focus on how you can learn to cope with the survivor's behavior during each stage of her recovery.

PART II

Coping with the Phases of Recovery

Chapter Four

Coping with Stage One:

Facing the Truth

As important as it is for you to understand the survivor and the recovery process, it is also important for you to learn ways of coping with the survivor's expectations and behaviors, many of which can push your own buttons and bring up issues from your own past. For each stage of recovery that the survivor goes through, you will need specific coping strategies.

COPING WITH THE SURVIVOR'S DISCLOSURE

Needless to say, learning for the first time that your mate, lover, or friend has suffered such a devastating trauma can be extremely upsetting. Bill, now a member of a prosurvivors' group, talked about how he reacted when his wife first told him about being abused:

"When Allison told me that her grandfather had had sex with her when she was a child, I felt as if someone had hit me in the stomach. I suddenly felt like I didn't know her at all. 'Who is this woman?' I thought. 'How could she have done such a thing?' I didn't see it at all from the perspective of her having been an innocent child. I just thought of her as this precocious child—a Lolita or something. I started wondering whether she had been faithful to me, whether I pleased her sexually or if she was comparing me with her grandfather. I realize now that my thinking was really screwed up. My male ego was so fragile that I thought of this creep as some kind of competition, like some old boyfriend of hers or something. I wasn't there for her at all. I was just thinking about myself."

This kind of reaction is not all that uncommon. Unfortunately, in our society we still tend to blame the victim, no matter what the crime. We still feel more comfortable with the idea that people bring things on themselves, that they invite adversity. This makes us all feel less afraid, less out of control. If we believed otherwise—that any of us can be victims of random crime, regardless of who we are or what we do—we would have to face our own vulnerability and mortality.

It is perfectly natural, of course, for you to have a strong reaction when the survivor first tells you about the abuse. Feelings of jealousy, disgust, fear, and anger are all understandable and common. You are a product of your environment, and as such you have been influenced by our society's ignorance about the subject of childhood sexual abuse. You may need to be reeducated about it, but that doesn't mean you are uncaring. Don't judge yourself for your feelings, no matter how inappropriate they may seem.

You need to have a place where you can talk openly about your feelings, no matter what they are, and a place where you can find the support you need. By joining a prosurvivors' group, you will have the chance to talk with other partners of survivors. You will be able to go beyond your initial reaction, whether it be jealousy, fear, anger, or disgust, and move on to a better understanding of why you reacted that way.

Depending on how you react to the survivor's disclosure, your relationship can either suffer greatly or improve. If you tend to react as Bill did and are having a hard time believing that the survivor was an innocent victim in the abuse, your relationship is at risk. As I have stated several times before, it is essential for the survivor to be believed and supported. If you continue to blame the survivor, she will feel abandoned and betrayed and may not even want to be around you. For this reason, it will be important for you to work on your feelings of disbelief in your prosurvivors' group and not share them with the survivor.

When the secret is finally out, a couple may be brought closer together. This was the case with Brenda and Josh. As Brenda described it:

"I love Josh so much, and it hurt me to hear that he had been violated in such a horrible way. I just held him for the longest time, and we both cried and cried. I don't think we have ever been as close as we were at that time. Since then it's as though an invisible barrier between us has been lifted. I think keeping that secret from me was really a strain on Josh. He told me he was afraid of how I'd react—he was afraid I'd think he was a freak, or homosexual, or something. But all I felt was love for him and pain because he had to suffer for so long all alone."

Learning about the abuse can also create more understanding between partners. As Morgan relayed to me:

"When Teresa finally told me about what had happened to her as a child, it made everything come together. Suddenly everything made sense—her nightmares, her inability to really get close to me, her being overprotective of our son. It was like being able to suddenly breathe a sigh of relief, because now I really understood my wife. She didn't seem so much like a stranger to me."

In the next few pages, we will discuss some of the most common reactions to survivors' disclosures.

WHEN YOU JUST CAN'T BELIEVE IT

When Monica told her friend Brooke that she had been molested by her father, Brooke had this reaction:

"I simply couldn't believe it. Monica's father is a *preacher,* and in my mind preachers don't do things like that to their children. Because Monica and her father never really got along and he had always been so harsh with her, I thought she was just making it up to get back at him. It devastated Monica that I didn't believe her. She told me it hurt her almost as much as the betrayal by her father. Now I realize I just didn't *want* to believe it because it shattered my image of preachers and other religious leaders. I'm a strongly religious person, and this information threatened to shake my faith."

James, the husband of my client Sylvia, had different reasons for not believing his wife's disclosure.

"This is the man I go golfing with every Saturday. This is the man who loaned me $10,000 to start my business. This is the man who takes us all out for dinner twice a month. How could I believe that this same man, a guy who has been like a second father to me, could have done such a thing? I'm ashamed now to say it, but when it came down to it, at first I chose my father-in-law over my wife. At the time I guess that in some ways he meant more to me than she did."

Fortunately, James was finally able to set his own needs aside and believe his wife, even though it was very painful for him. This meant that he lost his golf partner, because once he faced the truth about his father-in-law he was unable to be around him. Ultimately, James chose to believe his wife for his own well-being: *"I basically just couldn't live with myself. I knew somehow that I had sold out, that I was not only going against my wife but myself as well."*

The raw reality of childhood sexual abuse is so terrible that it is sometimes difficult to hear and thus to believe. Jordan, married to a male survivor, felt badly about her initial reaction:

"When my husband told me that his uncle had brutally raped him and forced him to perform oral sex on him, I told him I didn't believe him. The acts he was describing were so inhuman. How could I believe that anyone would do such things to a young boy? I accused him of hallucinating, since he had been heavily into drugs when he was a teenager. I know now that I hurt him terribly by not believing him."

Bear in mind that, barring mental illness, no one would willingly choose to say that she or he had been sexually abused as a child unless it were true, because being a victim of sexual abuse is just too humiliating and embarrassing. Only those who have actually been abused are willing to put themselves through the hell of recovery with all its accompanying pain, anger, and fear. By the time a survivor is sure enough of what happened to tell you about it, you'd better believe she is not making it up for shock value, to get attention, or to get back at someone who has hurt her. There are far easier ways to do this than to expose herself to gossip and pity and to risk permanently alienating herself from her family.

If you still have a hard time believing a survivor even though you want to, look at your own history for signs that you yourself may have been abused and are in denial (an unconscious defense mechanism that enables us to block out of our memory events that are traumatic or unpleasant).

People in denial about their own experience of sexual abuse often have the hardest time believing the disclosures of others.

"WHY DIDN'T SHE TELL ME BEFORE?"

Some partners and friends feel betrayed and angry with survivors who have waited a long time to tell their secret. The prosurvivor may feel as if he never really knew his partner, or that she had no right to keep such a thing from him. Vincent stayed angry with his wife for quite some time.

"I was angry and hurt because it made me feel like my wife didn't trust me and love me enough to share such an important part of her life with me. I just couldn't understand how she could have kept something like that from me for so long."

It is confusing to us when someone suddenly "remembers" an event or events that happened many years ago. How can someone have such a total memory lapse?

Children who are sexually abused are under high degrees of both physical and emotional stress. They are flooded with intense feelings of pain, fear, panic, anger, and betrayal—feelings they are emotionally unequipped to handle. Being forced to submit to the will of the abuser robs the child of any sense of control over her or his own experience. When no other help is available, victims frequently rely on indirect methods of coping. These methods of self-protection are called defense mechanisms.

The most common defense mechanism is a process known as *dissociation,* in which victims "blank out" or mentally divorce themselves from their experiences. Some victims dissociate by concentrating all their awareness on something else while the abuse is occurring—for example, a part of their own body that is not being invaded, sounds outside the room, a spot on the ceiling. This intense concentration can take them completely away from the horrifying experience at hand. Although dissociation helps victims to survive the abuse, it can also cause them to either lose all memory of the experience or to have only a vague, dreamlike recall of it. This may then cause victims to end up believing that the event did not really happen.

Because of this kind of dissociation process, many victims are able to remember the abuse only when a certain object, smell, color, scene, or experience triggers a sudden, severe reaction. This involuntary mental replay of a previous, vivid experience is called a flashback.

Not remembering the abuse is not the only reason survivors may not mention it for years. Some have always remembered the abuse but are so afraid of telling their partners about it that they put it off, sometimes for years. Priscilla had been married for ten years before she was finally able to tell her husband about her sexual abuse:

"I was afraid to tell my husband that I had been molested by my brother, because I was afraid he would get turned off to me. The acts my brother performed on me were so disgusting that I assumed my husband would find *me* disgusting. I wanted to tell him right away, when we first started dating, and I always felt dishonest about not telling him, but I was just too afraid and ashamed. Finally, I just couldn't keep it to myself any longer.

"As it turned out, my husband did have quite a few problems with it at first. Because my brother was only a few years older than I was, my husband didn't really see it as abuse. He thought I had wanted it, too, and this really hurt my feelings. It's taken some time, but now my husband understands that I was just an innocent victim and that I was afraid of my brother. Even though it's been painful, I am still glad that I told him. Since I don't have anything to hide from him and don't have to live in fear anymore of how he'll react when he finds out, I feel a lot closer to him now."

Jessica had similar reasons for not telling her boyfriend of three years:

"When I was younger, I had boyfriends who ended up treating me really differently when I told them about the abuse. Some treated me like a tramp or thought I was open to kinky sex, while others got turned off sexually. I decided I wasn't going to tell a guy right away, that the only guy I was going to tell was my future husband. Then the time came when I was going to get married, and I knew I should tell my fiancé, but I just kept putting it off. Then, when we were married, I convinced myself that it really didn't matter. Before I knew it, it had been 10 years, and I still hadn't told my husband."

Many male survivors are afraid to tell their partners because of the tremendous amount of shame that they carry at having been abused. This was the case with Hugh:

"I felt very ashamed about my sexual abuse, and I was afraid my girlfriend was going to think I was gay because my perpetrator was a male. When I finally got up enough nerve to tell her she was really nice about it, and very sympathetic. I was surprised, because I'd just assumed she wouldn't be able to understand. She made it really clear to me that she knew I'd been an innocent victim, and she said it hurt her to know that I had been hurt so much."

Other survivors are reluctant to tell because they are afraid their lovers or mates will become violent toward the perpetrator. As Marsha explained,

"I was afraid of what Dan was going to do. He had a terrible temper, and I was afraid that he'd fly off the handle and try to kill my father. When I finally did tell him, I made him promise he wouldn't do anything to my father. He agreed, reluctantly, even though he wanted to beat him up."

Unfortunately, Veronica's husband, Tony, didn't exhibit as much control. As he told me,

"Veronica had been afraid of how I would react, and as it turned out she had good reason to be. When she finally did tell me I acted like a complete idiot. I became so enraged when my wife told me about her father that I stormed out of the house and drove like a maniac over to her parents' home. I grabbed him by the collar, told him he was a lousy son-of-a-bitch, and proceeded to pound the hell out of him. My wife arrived a few minutes later in a panic, crying hysterically. Her father was all right, but she wasn't. She was so upset that she had to be taken to the hospital and given a sedative. Not only was I no comfort to her when she needed me, but I added to her problems by scaring her to death."

Other survivors feel it is important to tell prospective partners or friends about their sexual abuse early on in the relationship. Some feel they owe it to a potential mate to let him or her know what they are getting into. Geneva told the members of her recovery group why she told her boyfriend right away:

"I decided to tell him about the sexual abuse as soon as we started getting serious. I had had several years of therapy already, but I knew that it would still be a while before I recovered. I also knew that in some respects I would never be over the damage, and that anyone I married would have to adjust to certain behaviors on my part that might be difficult to cope with. I didn't think it was fair to get seriously involved with someone without letting him know about this important part of my life."

Still others use telling their secret as a way of testing the new partner or friend to see how she or he will react. This was the case with Ryan, a male survivor who had been molested by an older neighborhood boy.

"Once I finally understood on both an emotional and an intellectual level that the sexual abuse was not my fault, I no longer felt ashamed of it or had any need to hide it. I decided to tell the women that I dated about the abuse right away to see how they reacted. If a woman changed toward me and acted like I was a freak or something, then I just never asked her out again. I was tired of being treated like it was my fault or like there was something wrong with me. I've met lots of women who are very understanding about it, and many of them have ended up telling me that they were abused, too."

Friends and lovers can sometimes get angry when they realize that they are being "tested" by being told about the abuse. This was the case with Jeff:

"When we first started dating, Mary Jane told me that she had been sexually molested by a family friend. I told her at the time that I felt bad for her, but that I certainly didn't hold it against her in any way. This seemed to make her feel good about me right away, but I noticed that she continued to bring it up at certain times, always testing how I was going to react.

"For example, when she first met my parents she ended up telling them right away also. I felt pretty uncomfortable about this because it just seemed so inappropriate. I told her I wished she had waited a little while, and she took this as evidence that I was ashamed of her. No matter how I tried to assure her that I wasn't, she just wouldn't believe me. Finally, I just came to the conclusion that with time she was going to either believe me or she wasn't, and that there was basically nothing I could do to force her to trust me."

It is very common for survivors to test, and to keep on testing, their partners and friends. While you certainly have a right to get angry about this, try to remember why it is so difficult for the survivor to trust. Doing as Jeff did, realizing that you can't persuade the survivor to trust you until she is ready, is probably the best way to go.

HOW COULD SHE HAVE LET IT HAPPEN?

A child who is sexually abused has absolutely no responsibility for the abuse. Even if the child wasn't forced or didn't protest, even if she didn't tell, even if she continued to have a sexual relationship with the perpetrator after the abuse, or even if she or he came to derive some physical pleasure from the stimulation, it is always the responsibility of the adult not to be sexual with a child. No child seduces an abuser. Children ask for attention and affection, not for sexual abuse.

Implying or stating that the survivor was responsible for the sexual abuse or must have asked for it in some way only reinforces her already intense feelings of irrational guilt and sense of worthlessness. The following insinuations, couched as questions, are examples of blaming the victim:

"Why didn't she or he tell someone?"

Most children are afraid to tell anyone about the sexual abuse for numerous reasons, including the following:

- ➤ They have been threatened by the perpetrator, whom they fear may hurt or even kill them, their parents, someone else they care about, or even their pets.
- ➤ They are afraid no one will believe them. They may have already had the experience of telling their parents the truth about something else, only to be accused of making it up. Many children feel that their word alone would very likely not be believed.
- ➤ They are afraid they will be blamed.
- ➤ They are afraid they will be punished. Children who are sexually abused often have a history of being severely punished for even the slightest mistake. They are therefore much more inclined to keep quiet about something so awful, which is bound to result in commensurate punishment.
- ➤ They feel there is no use in telling. If their parents are rarely around or are usually overly involved in their own lives, children may feel that their parents simply don't care what happens to them.
- ➤ They feel such guilt and shame that they just can't tell. This is especially true if their bodies responded to the sexual stimulation. They fear that anyone they might tell would surely blame them as much as they blame themselves.
- ➤ They feel that somehow their mother must already know about what is going on, and therefore they feel too betrayed by her to tell.
- ➤ They feel their mother knows and interpret her inaction as silent permission.
- ➤ They may be afraid that their mother would divorce their father (the abuser) if they told. Many victims fear being sent to a foster home.

➤ They may be protecting the perpetrator, keeping the secret for the sake of a parent or another person they care about.

"Why did she/he keep going back for more?"

Children often continue to be around the perpetrator because they are getting some of their other needs met—needs that are not being met elsewhere—such as attention, holding, affection, and compliments. Children do not go back for the sex. In fact, most survivors just put up with the sex, often dissociating or splitting off from themselves in order to withstand it.

"What if she/he derived some sexual pleasure from it?"

Some victims of childhood sexual abuse talk about how their bodies betrayed them because they responded to the sexual stimulation even though they were afraid, hurt, or repulsed by the acts. Unfortunately, our bodies can respond without our consent.

"What if the child was old enough to know better?"

No matter what age a child is, or how clever or mature, she or he is never a match for an adult. An adult doesn't have to use physical force or threats to control his victim. He has such power over a child, merely by being an adult, that most children are afraid of him. Children are taught to obey what adults tell them. They learn that if they don't want to be punished, or if they want to be loved, they'd better do what they are told. Most child molesters are great con artists and are able to manipulate children into doing whatever they want them to do.

The actions are considered to be sexual abuse if the child was coerced, deceived, threatened, bribed, or intimidated. When sexual encounters are not based on mutual consent, they always constitute assault.

A child under the age of 18 is not old enough to "consent" to having sex with an adult or even with an older child, because there is a difference in power. For true consent, an individual must know what it is that she or he is consenting to and must have the freedom to say yes or no. Children and most adolescents lack both the information necessary to make an "informed" decision about the matter and the personal freedom, power, or position to say yes or no to an adult, especially if that adult controls all their means for survival. The average age of children who are sexually abused is between 9 and 13. Few people would consider a child of such an age to be old enough to be responsible for her or his own decisions, *particularly* in the area of sexuality.

Generally, children under the age of 16, and sometimes older, are not emotionally equipped to have sex with anyone, much less with an adult or a much older adolescent. In addition, if the person attempting to have sex with the child is a parent or parental figure, an older sibling, or any other family member, the child is not in the position to "know better" but instead is being unduly influenced by someone she or he loves and is dependent upon.

"Why are some children victimized over and over by several different perpetrators? They must be doing something to attract the abuse."

Perpetrators "pick" whoever is available and convenient, often choosing children who are most vulnerable. They have an uncanny knack for singling out children who have already been victimized in some way (physically, verbally, or emotionally), and they can spot the child who is hungry for love, attention, and affection. Once a child has been sexually abused, she or he is an easy target for other child molesters. The previously victimized child has low self-esteem and tends to submit more willingly to advances.

The child who is protected and supervised properly by her family, especially by her mother, is not easy prey to child molesters. Children whose mothers are physically or psychologically absent are the most vulnerable. Those who live in isolated settings or who have few friends and social contacts are also at greater risk.

"Don't some children just ask for trouble?"

Children or adolescents never "ask for" sexual abuse, no matter how "seductive" they may seem to be in dress or in action.

Spend some time with children who are around the same age the survivor was when she was first molested. Notice how naïve and innocent they are. Do you think children of this age could ever really *want* sex with an adult? Do you think they are old enough for sex? No matter how sophisticated they may appear, it is easy to see that they are, in fact, very vulnerable.

Children who appear especially seductive or "sexy" have probably already been sexually abused. A previously victimized child may appear to be sexual in the way she stands, sits, or moves, or she may have learned to be seductive in order to get attention.

"But aren't there some cases where the child really **did** *want it, and may even have instigated it?"*

I repeat: a so-called precocious, provocative, or seductive child appears so only because of prior sexual abuse. This behavior reveals that the child has already been sexualized, that she has already been introduced to sex and has "learned" that acting seductive can be an effective way to get the affection, attention, and approval she so badly needs.

The perpetrator teaches his victims a powerful but dysfunctional message—that they are important because of their sexuality. Sex becomes a tool that is used to manipulate others. Ironically, however, these children are even more desperate for love after the abuse than they were before. Since most victims of childhood sexual abuse do not tell anyone about the trauma they have been through, there is no one to comfort them. They feel alone and scared, with nowhere to turn for solace. So they look for reassurance and comfort anywhere they can find it—even if it means being abused again (sometimes by the same person).

WHEN THE PERPETRATOR IS SOMEONE YOU'RE CLOSE TO

Not only does the survivor have complicated feelings toward the perpetrator, but you may, also. If the perpetrator is someone you have been close to, someone you may even love, it will be especially difficult for you to face the fact that this person could do such a reprehensible act and be responsible for such devastating damage in your partner. Even though you may believe your partner, it will still be difficult to face the truth. You may tend to minimize the damage caused or make excuses for the perpetrator (for instance, he was under a lot of stress, his wife must not have been giving him enough sex, he must have been abused himself as a child, and so on). Remember, no matter what his situation, no one has the right to take out his problems, anger, or pain on a helpless, innocent child.

I have often heard mates, family, and friends of survivors tell me that the perpetrator wasn't responsible for his actions because he was drunk at the time of the abuse or because he was in a blackout (an amnesia-like state during extreme intoxication, with the alcoholic later having little or no recall of events and of his actions during that time). But no matter how drunk the perpetrator was, he is still responsible for his actions. Making an excuse for a perpetrator based on the idea that he was drunk is like saying that a drunk driver who kills someone while driving isn't responsible for his actions because he was drunk.

Some of the perpetrators I have treated who are alcoholics have admitted to me that they had sexual fantasies and thoughts about children long before they ever abused a child. The alcohol did not create in them the desire to molest a child, but instead lowered their inhibitions so that this unhealthy part of them could temporarily take over.

Another argument I frequently hear against holding the perpetrator responsible for his actions is that so many perpetrators were themselves sexually abused as children and are just repeating the cycle of abuse. While we know this is true in a large majority of cases, this still does not excuse their behavior. There are many people who were victims of sexual abuse who do not become child molesters themselves. Many have sought professional help because they became aware that they had such tendencies, and some refuse to be around children for these very reasons.

While perpetrators who were victims of sexual abuse certainly deserve our sympathy and understanding, especially if they are willing to admit their problem and willing to seek professional help, we still cannot excuse their behavior. Again, not holding them responsible for their behavior is like not prosecuting a murderer because he came from an abusive home: while we can understand what led to his violence, we must hold him accountable for his behavior and make certain that he does not kill again.

Remember, perpetrators are very good at eliciting sympathy for their point of view. They seldom take responsibility for their actions, and instead they usually blame others for "making" them do whatever it is they have done that is considered negative by others. Your partner or friend has had to work long and hard, and will have to continue to do so, in order to fully comprehend that she was not responsible for the sexual abuse and that she has the right to be angry at the perpetrator. If you sympathize with the abuser, it will confuse the survivor and make her doubt her own perceptions once again, make her doubt whether she should be angry at the perpetrator, or cause her to feel angry and hurt because you are taking the abuser's side.

It is essential that you do not in any way defend the perpetrator in front of your partner, even if you feel an allegiance toward him or her. Take this issue to your prosurvivors' group, where you can talk openly about your confusion and about your love or loyalty for the perpetrator or for your partner's family. Do not, however, talk to the survivor about your confusion. She should not have to be put in the position of having to convince you that she has a right to her anger or that you should be angry with the perpetrator.

The survivor needs your absolute loyalty. No matter how close you are to the abuser, no matter how hard a life the abuser has had, your sympathies need to be with the victim, not the perpetrator. If you defend the actions of the abuser in any way, the survivor will see this as a betrayal.

Some people have tried to pressure their lover or friend into forgiving the perpetrator or other abusive family members so that everything can "go back to the way it was" before the disclosure. This may be because they view the perpetrator or other family members as surrogate parents or just because, like Lyle, he or she is uncomfortable with adversity of any kind:

"I'm just the kind of person who can't stand conflict of any kind. When my friend told me that his brother had sexually abused him, I felt bad for him and was as supportive as I could possibly be. But now I feel it's time for him to forgive and forget. After all, it was a long time ago, and they were both kids at the time. But my friend is making a big deal out of this, and he says he can't forgive his brother until he admits that he abused him and apologizes to him. I know his brother is never going to do this, so why belabor the point? Let's just go on with our lives—why continue to cause upset over something that happened so long ago?"

It is not fair of you to pressure someone else into forgiving, or to try to make her feel guilty over maintaining a certain stance. Unless you yourself were sexually abused as a child, you do not know how it feels to have gone through what she has. Most abusers do not admit the abuse, do not apologize, and do not ask for forgiveness. This makes it very difficult for the survivor to forgive him. In addition, there is no shame in not forgiving; few people ever really complete the task, even when they want to. Forgiveness is certainly not necessary for recovery, and for many, "forgiveness" without the full recovery process can be used as a way of denying and pretending that nothing ever happened.

As much as you may want things to be the way they were before the disclosure, this is not possible. Everything has changed for the survivor since her acknowledgment of the sexual abuse. And if she has been able to confront the perpetrator and her family of origin about the abuse, nothing will ever be the same for them, either. Even more important for you, as much as you try to deny that this devastating event has touched your life, it has. You now know that someone you love was hurt in a very profound way. You now realize that your partner or friend has been damaged in ways that have severely affected not only her life, but yours as well. No amount of denial, no amount of forgiveness will make things go back to the way they were. You, the survivor, and the survivor's family are irreparably changed. Fortunately, this change will be for the good. Even though you will not be able to see it now, the fact that your partner or friend has admitted the truth and come out of denial will mean that her life will be improved greatly. This in turn can make your relationship better.

Chapter Five

Coping with Stages Two and Three: Releasing Anger, and Confronting the Abuser and Others

At the same time that your partner or friend is learning to express her anger constructively, you will also need to do so. Discovering that someone you care so much about was hurt in such a way will likely make you angry at the perpetrator, the silent partner, and anyone else who didn't protect or believe the survivor as a child. In addition, prosurvivors are in some ways indirect victims of the abuse and therefore feel angry at the perpetrator. Some partners are even angry at society for allowing childhood sexual abuse to occur in the first place. All of these reactions are understandable.

YOUR ANGER AT THE PERPETRATOR AND OTHER MEMBERS OF THE SURVIVOR'S FAMILY

While the desire to unload your rage on the perpetrator is understandable, it is rarely a good idea to act on this desire. If you find that you are having difficulty controlling your urges to lash out at the perpetrator, you will need to find constructive ways of dealing with your anger. Just talking it out with someone might help. Prosurvivors' groups are often the best place to express your anger, since there you will find other people who identify with your feelings and a safe environment in which to express your anger.

Some partners of survivors feel that it is their place to confront the perpetrator. As George, whose wife had been brutally raped by her father, explained,

"I felt that as a man, I should stand up to my wife's father and let him know that I knew what he had done and that if he ever came near Grace again, I'd hurt him badly. I felt like it was my role to protect my wife against anyone who had hurt her or could hurt her in the future. But she explained to me that it wasn't my place to do this at all, but hers. She said that my reaction showed my old-fashioned way of thinking that a husband's role was that of protector. She told me that she had to fight her own battles and not rely on me. What she said made a lot of sense to me, even though I still tend to feel it's the husband's role to protect his wife and family."

It is *not* your place to confront the perpetrator. This would amount to "taking care" of your partner in a way that actually denies her control of the situation. The survivor needs to be the one to do the confronting, if and when it is to happen.

Philip, a client of mine married to a survivor, explained how he felt about his wife's brother, who had been her abuser.

"I wanted to retaliate for all the damage he had done to her. I guess I believe in "an eye for an eye," and I felt like a wimp just standing by while this creep got away with it. But my wife told me that she didn't blame her brother, that she realized he was just a victim of the same horrible family she was. I tried to explain to her that he still had no right to take his anger out on her like that. She told me that she needed time to sort it all out in her mind and that she wanted me to stay out of it."

As I told Philip, it is important to realize that survivors have very complicated feelings toward the perpetrator and for that matter, toward their entire family of origin, and they do need time to sort those feelings out. While the perpetrator certainly caused tremendous damage, he may also have been the only person in the survivor's childhood who was kind and affectionate toward her. This is frequently true of father/daughter incest when the mother is unaffectionate, distant, and emotionally unavailable, but the father is affectionate toward his daughter and is involved in her life.

Survivors typically change their feelings toward the perpetrator and the family of origin several times during their recovery. They may deny the full extent of what really happened to them for quite some time, trying desperately to hold onto their illusion that the perpetrator loved them and that they had a normal, loving family. They may then begin to feel some anger toward those who hurt them and become enraged, only to slip back into denial again, especially around holidays and special occasions. It is a tremendously difficult task to come to terms with the fact that those you thought loved you were, in fact, using and abusing you. And it is terribly painful to let go of a parent or the fantasy of a loving parent.

It often takes time for a survivor to tap into her anger at the perpetrator. As mentioned many times, you will need to give your partner the necessary time and space to get in touch with just how angry she is. This doesn't mean, however, that you have to wait for her in order to express your own anger. While you don't want to traumatize her by going after the perpetrator, and you don't want to overwhelm her with your rage, your anger is appropriate and justified. In fact, seeing the prosurvivor expressing his anger toward the perpetrator or others involved can give the survivor permission to feel her own anger. This was the case with Virginia:

"I hadn't been able to get in touch with my anger toward my father for molesting me because I love him so much. But when Andy told me how furious he was at my father, how enraged he was at him for hurting me so much, something in me just snapped. Hearing Andy get angry suddenly gave me permission to feel my own anger. I began to tell Andy about how really angry I was, too. Then I jumped up and tore up this huge pillow we had on the floor, all the while yelling and telling off my father. Andy kept spurring me on by yelling things like, 'Yeah, take that, you bastard.' The more angry he became, the more angry I became. It felt great."

Showing your anger can also show your partner how much you love her or him. This is what happened with Pete:

"When I saw how angry Charles got when I told him how my grandfather had molested me, it made me feel very loved. I had never experienced anyone becoming so angry at someone just because that person had hurt me. It was as though my grandfather had hurt Charles, too, when he hurt me. That blew me away."

There are many ways to release your anger in indirect, constructive ways. If you feel as if you need to ventilate your anger in a physical way, use a punching bag, or hit your bed, couch, or a large pillow with a plastic or foam bat, an old tennis racket, a folded-up newspaper, or a rolled-up towel. Place a picture of the abuser on the spot that you are going to hit, or imagine the perpetrator's face as you do your hitting.

Another way to express your anger is to imagine that you are having a conversation with the perpetrator. Tell him everything you want to say, holding nothing back. Or put your face in a pillow and yell as loudly as you can.

Many prosurvivors have found that writing a letter or making a tape recording in which they tell the perpetrator exactly how they feel has helped them immensely. While most have found that the exercise of writing the letter or making the recording is release enough, some have actually chosen to mail the letter or tape. If you stick to your own feelings about what the perpetrator did and how it has affected your relationship with your partner, it is not the same as taking care of the survivor or doing her confronting for her.

The following is a letter written by the wife of a survivor to his father, the abuser. She did not send this letter but used it as a way of releasing her rage at her father-in-law without having to censor what she wanted to say.

> Dear Paul:
>
> When I think of what you did to your son, my husband, I want to throw up. How you can hold your head up after doing such a despicable thing is beyond me. I think you should be tarred and feathered the way they used to punish

people in the old days, then put in the town square with a sign on you saying "CHILD MOLESTER" or, better yet, "CHILD RAPIST."

But now that I think of it, that doesn't seem punishment enough for all the pain you caused Joel. No punishment seems to be good enough for you. You are slime, the lowest of the low. You don't deserve to be on this earth, since you are barely human. I hope to God that you will be punished in the worst way possible. I hope he makes you burn in hell, or that you get some horrible disease and that you suffer in pain for years and years before dying a painful death.

I hate you for having hurt Joel the way you did, for violating him and then lying about it, for going on with your life as if nothing had ever happened. I have lost all respect for you as a man. I once admired you, but now all I feel is disgust when I think of you. You are a pathetic excuse for a human being and I don't want anything more to do with you. I don't want to have to see your face ever again and be reminded of the horrible things you did to your own innocent child.

Rick, the husband of a survivor, decided to mail the letter he wrote to his wife's abuser, her father:

Dear Simon:

Hope has told me recently about the fact that you sexually abused her for several years, starting when she was eight years old. First of all, I want you to know that I believe her. Secondly, I want you to know how I feel about what you have done. You probably don't have any idea how very much you have hurt Hope, how much you have damaged her life. I will leave this up to her to tell you when she is ready. I will tell you, however, how you molesting your daughter has affected me.

Because you violated Hope in the worst possible way, our marriage has suffered. Because you betrayed her she is unable to trust anyone, even me. I have had the extremely difficult task of trying to convince her that not all men are like her father, that some can be trusted and some can be unselfish.

Because you abused your *very* own daughter I have had to question myself to see if I am capable of the same thing. Although I feel no such desire, I have lost trust in myself. I

> fear that if I become too physically close to my daughter I will succumb to some unknown madness within myself and hurt her the way you hurt Hope. This has caused me to be overcautious, to push my daughter away at times, to appear to be unloving. I know this has hurt her tremendously but I hope to be able to get close to her again in the future.
>
> You will probably never fully know how much your selfishness has damaged my family. By sexually abusing your daughter you violated me as well. Be assured that I will not allow you to have any access to my daughter and run the risk of your violating her as well.

While some of these anger-releasing techniques may sound bizarre to you, they are actually time-honored therapeutic techniques that are designed to help you release your anger constructively without hurting anyone and without producing guilt.

If your anger seems to get out of hand, if it doesn't subside after you have worked on finding constructive ways of releasing it toward the perpetrator, it may be an indication that your anger is not just about your partner's or friend's sexual abuse but may have to do with some issues of your own. Spend some time thinking about when you most often get angry and what issues bring up that anger. Try to discover whether there is anything in your own past that parallels your mate's or friend's situation. You may want to seek out the help of a professional therapist to help you get to the root of your anger.

YOUR ANGER AT SOCIETY

One of the best ways of releasing anger at the injustices of society is to become actively involved in changing the system. Many a movement was started because someone needed a way to deal with anger over an injustice that affected her or him personally. For example, Candy Lightner, founder of Mothers Against Drunk Driving (MADD), started that organization after her child was killed by a drunk driver.

Become involved in activities that support childhood sexual abuse victims, such as donating time or money to help abused children. Or become politically involved in working toward making child molesters pay for the therapy of their victims and serve longer sentences, or in improving the type of treatment they receive.

YOUR ANGER AT THE SURVIVOR

Sooner or later, you are bound to get tired of being patient, understanding, and supportive. Whether you get tired of having your life constantly disrupted by the survivor's outbursts, mood shifts, or demands, or of her pushing you away or mistrusting you, it is inevitable that you will lose your cool now and then.

As noted earlier, survivors tend to focus a lot of their anger on those closest to them. However, as difficult as this may be to understand, it will only complicate things and will probably damage your relationship if you strike out at the survivor directly. Try sharing your frustration with others in your prosurvivors' group or using one of the constructive anger-release techniques.

You may also want to try talking to the survivor at a time when you are both calm. Tell her how it feels when she treats you as though you were the enemy. She needs to be aware of how her actions make you feel so that she can begin to work on making a distinction between the past and the present. You may find that eventually, even in the heat of anger, you will be able to remind her that you are *not* the abuser, and that you are not going to hurt her. This kind of statement can do a lot to squelch your own anger and hers as well.

Just because you don't allow yourself to yell and scream at the survivor doesn't mean that you are repressing your feelings. It just means that you are practicing restraint, suppressing your emotions until you can find a constructive outlet for them.

From time to time you may also feel angry because you and your mate or lover can't lead a "normal" life but must instead always have to be coping with the effects of the abuse. Doug, whose wife has been in therapy for two years, complained:

"I just get so angry sometimes that we have to live like this. Other people don't have to cope with the kinds of things we have to—flashbacks, Kelly's intense fear that something will happen to our children, our kids not being able to see their grandparents, and our not being able to have sex for months on end. What a way to live!"

It is truly very frustrating to have to cope constantly with problems that you never bargained for. Allow yourself to feel your frustration and anger, ventilating your feelings by talking to a friend or to members of your support group, writing in your journal, or talking into a tape recorder. Don't allow your anger to build up too much before finding a constructive way of ventilating it. Communicating calmly with your partner when you have reached your tolerance level and *before* you have reached the saturation point helps to prevent your anger from building up.

Of course, no matter how hard you try, there will be times when you've had enough—when you can't take one more rejection, one more outburst from your partner, one more time when your lovemaking is interrupted by one of her flashbacks. It is humanly impossible for you to be understanding, patient, and supportive at all times.

Earl sheepishly confessed to members of his support group how angry he gets at his girlfriend:

"Sometimes I just don't think I can stand another night of hearing Claudia crying or of being awakened by her nightmares. I feel bad for her, of course, and I really want to be there for her, but I need my sleep so I can go to work in the morning. I hate to admit it, but sometimes I just lose it and tell her to shut up or to leave me alone. I feel guilty about it the next morning, but at the time it feels like I just can't take one more sleepless night."

You and your partner or friend both need to understand that while you are working hard to understand her and the recovery process and are making an effort to be as patient as possible, you are not a saint. She may need to be reminded from time to time that while you love her, you have needs of your own.

Members of Earl's group let him know that they understood his predicament and that he didn't need to feel guilty about getting angry sometimes. They also talked about the necessity of setting limits to avoid getting to the point of becoming angry. For example, if Earl had let Claudia know up front that he was beginning to feel stressed out from too many sleepless nights and that he needed his sleep, the couple might have been able to work something out. They might have decided to sleep in different rooms for a few nights until he caught up on his sleep. Or, perhaps Earl could have comforted Claudia for a few minutes after a nightmare but then gone back to sleep, with Claudia going into another room to calm down. We will deal more with the issue of setting limits in later chapters. For now, just keep in mind that it can short-circuit your anger.

It's also important to make sure that you aren't taking your anger at the perpetrator out on the survivor. Eleanor, the wife of a survivor, realized that she was doing just that:

"There was a time when I felt very angry with Bud, but I didn't know why. I'd end up yelling at him for no apparent reason, and then I'd feel really bad about it because I knew he was going through such a rough time. When I talked about it in my group, someone suggested that maybe I was getting mad at Bud instead of focusing my anger on his mother, who had abused him. As soon as the words were out of her mouth I knew she was right. That was *exactly* what I had been doing."

Throughout the survivor's recovery, there will be many times when your own anger will surface. Each time you see the person you care about rejected or blamed by her family of origin, each time you hear her cry over the tremendous pain brought on by memories of the abuse, each time she gets in touch with another layer of pain, fear, or anger, you will likely experience your anger at the perpetrator or the family all over again.

Working on releasing your anger constructively can benefit both you and your relationship. Although it may be difficult at times to give yourself permission to feel and express your anger, if you can work past any preconceived ideas that anger is a negative emotion that should be repressed and avoided, you will begin to recognize how very beneficial its constructive release can be.

Chapter Six

Coping with Stage Four:

Resolving Family Relationships

As noted earlier, the survivor's decisions regarding her relationships with the perpetrator and with her family are hers alone to make. No one but the survivor herself can know whether continuing a relationship with the perpetrator or with family members who didn't protect her is the best thing for her or not.

This doesn't mean that you won't get angry with her from time to time for vacillating in her decisions or for making what you consider a "wrong" decision. However, instead of sharing your feelings with your mate or friend, try to deal with your anger by finding constructive ways to release it.

TO SEE . . .

Some survivors continue to see the perpetrator, and this is sometimes difficult for their partner to understand. Timothy, a prosurvivor and a client of mine, objected:

"I just can't believe Leslie still wants to see her father. He sexually abused her, for God's sake! You'd think she couldn't stand to be around him another minute. I don't understand the hold he still has on her. Every time she sees him she's a basket case afterward, but she still insists on going over there every weekend."

Timothy, like many people, did not understand the strong need many survivors have to try to win their parents' love, even when those parents have been abusive. With some education about the dynamics of childhood sexual abuse, Timothy came to understand his wife better and became less critical of her.

While in therapy, Timothy also learned to manage his own needs better. He decided that while he no longer felt critical of his wife for continuing to see her parents, he himself did not feel comfortable being around them. He took care of himself by telling his wife that he was no longer willing to go with her when she visited them.

You, too, will need to decide for yourself how much involvement you wish to have with the survivor's family. For example, you don't have to continue making weekly visits to your in-laws' house, pretending that everything is fine. You can stay home while your wife continues to make her weekly visits, or you can ask your wife to compromise and stay home with you every other week. You don't have to smile and pretend that you like the survivor's brother, who not only sexually abused her as a child but continues to be obnoxious and abusive to everyone around him. You can either refuse to be around him any longer or let your partner know that from now on, you are going to confront him about his present abusive behavior. (Make sure that if you do so you focus on what the person does that bothers you now, as opposed to confronting him about his sexual abuse of the survivor, which would be interfering with the survivor's recovery.) You do not have to subject yourself to the pretense, humiliation, or danger of being around people who are hypercritical or abusive.

. . . OR NOT TO SEE

On the other hand, your partner or friend may decide either to temporarily separate from or even to "divorce" the perpetrator, those members of her family who still don't believe her, those who didn't protect her when she was a child, or those who are not willing to support her in the ways she needs for her recovery. Regardless of your feelings about this, you will need to go along with her decision. Continuing to relate to someone who abused your partner or who minimizes or denies the abuse, *no matter how close you are to that person,* would be a betrayal to your partner. Most survivors stop seeing their parents or siblings not as a way to punish them or to teach them a lesson, but solely as an act of self-preservation.

If you are married to a survivor and you have children, your spouse may decide that not only is she going to sever her own ties with certain family members, but that she doesn't want the children around them, either. You may feel that it is unfair of your partner to deprive your children of their grandparents, great-grandparents, aunts and uncles, or any other member of your spouse's family she or he has decided to stop seeing. Nevertheless, you need to support your partner in her decision. Do not attempt to sabotage her by arguing with her about it, trying to pressure her into changing her mind by making her feel guilty of depriving your children of their family, sneaking the children over to see the family, and so on.

Most survivors do not want their children around their families of origin if there is any possibility that the children will be negatively affected by the same abusive family members. This is a very valid concern, for we know that abusive people do not readily change. Unless the abuser has acknowledged his abusive behavior and either received psychological help for his problems or joined a support group that focuses on recovery from these problems (such as Parents Anonymous for abusive parents, Parents United for sexually abusive parents, or Alcoholics Anonymous), he is very likely to be abusive to your children in much the same way he was to your partner.

Even though you may feel that your children are not safe with your partner's parents or siblings, your partner may not be able to break away from her family. While you can't force your mate to stop seeing her abusive parents or siblings, you *can* take a strong stand against having your children be around them. Try explaining to your spouse just why it is that you disapprove of the children's having any contact with her family. Continue to try to make her understand. If she still refuses to agree, insist that her family see the children only when either you or she is with them, and that the children should never be alone with the abuser.

Chapter Seven

Coping with Stages Five and Six: Self-Discovery and Self-Care

During Stages Five and Six of her recovery, your partner or friend will very likely be preoccupied with discovering exactly who she is and exploring ways of taking better care of herself. As mentioned earlier, this may make you feel as though she is ignoring you or not spending enough time with you. While your tendency may be to get angry and insist that she spend more time with you, or to feel hurt and tell her she is not being a good lover or friend, your time could be far better spent in doing for yourself exactly what she is doing for herself—discovering yourself and learning how to better take care of *yourself.*

LEARNING TO FOCUS ON YOURSELF INSTEAD OF ONLY ON THE SURVIVOR

Partners of survivors often focus all their attention on the problems of the survivor and fail to deal with their own issues. It is always much easier to deal with another person's problems, and it is easier to recognize what others need to do in order to change. But you must now begin to put the focus back on yourself. In focusing so much of your attention on your partner or friend, you have probably neglected your own needs. You may have neglected your career, your family, your body, and, most importantly, your emotional well-being.

We all have emotional problems, and it is no coincidence that partners of survivors of sexual abuse sometimes seem to have more than their share. Perhaps it is because survivors tend to become attracted to partners whose backgrounds are similar to theirs, with alcoholic, neglectful, or abusive families of origin. One reason for this attraction is that there is such a sense of comfort and immediate rapport with those from similar circumstances.

You will need to ask yourself whether you are projecting your own needs onto your partner. Often, we give to others the nurturing, understanding, and support that we ourselves are so desperate for. This is often the case with prosurvivors who were themselves deprived, neglected, or abused as children.

In addition to joining a prosurvivors' group, you may want to enter individual psychotherapy. There are undoubtedly issues from your own past that get in your way, unfinished business with parents and other significant people that you need to complete. You need to focus on healing from your own childhood, and you can't get this healing by taking care of others.

Twelve-Step programs such as Al-Anon (for mates and families of alcoholics), ACA (Adult Children of Alcoholics), or CODA (Co-dependents Anonymous) can help prosurvivors learn to stop focusing all their attention on their partners and instead work on their own recovery.

You may also want to begin a self-improvement program in which you focus on your body and your health. This is always a good place to start, since most of us can stand some improvement in these areas and because the rewards are so immediate and ego-enhancing. Starting an exercise program, even if it is just taking a walk every day, will make you feel better about yourself and will relieve some of the stress you have been under. It's also a great way to work off excess sexual energy.

Knowing that your partner will be focusing a great deal of her time and attention on her recovery for quite some time, why not plan on going back to school, taking up a hobby or sport, or doing anything else that you have always wanted to do? Instead of seeing yourself as a victim because your partner isn't spending enough time with you, view this time as an opportunity for you to focus on yourself for a while.

THE PROBLEM OF CO-DEPENDENCY

One of the many issues you can focus on while your partner or friend is in recovery is co-dependency. As mentioned earlier, prosurvivors tend to be what are commonly termed *co-dependents,* or people who focus on the feelings, wants, and needs of others as a way to avoid dealing with their own lives. Because their energy and attention are directed away from self-discovery and self-care, many co-dependents stay stuck while their partners (the survivors) get healthier. Many a recovered survivor has ended a relationship with a co-dependent friend or lover because the survivor has, in a sense, outgrown the other person.

A co-dependent has a pattern of getting involved with people whom he or she tries to rescue or take care of. In fact, if you are a co-dependent, this may not be the first relationship you have had with a survivor or someone else who has a problem such as drinking, drugs, compulsive gambling, and so on. By getting involved with people who have these or other problems, such as an inability to become intimate, sexual problems, or abusive behavior, a co-dependent can always blame his or her unhappiness on the mate's problems. Also, since the partner has obvious problems, the co-dependent person's own inadequacies can be overlooked. And while the co-dependent is just as dependent on the relationship as the survivor is, he or she is better able to maintain the illusion of being in control and on top of things.

The irony is that as much as co-dependents feel responsible for others and take care of others, deep down they believe that other people are somehow responsible for *them.* They blame others for their unhappiness and their problems, and they feel that if it weren't for those other people, they would be happy.

Another irony is that while the co-dependent feels controlled by people and events, he is himself overly controlling. He is afraid of allowing other people to be who they are and of allowing events to happen naturally. An expert in knowing best how things should turn out and how people should behave, the co-dependent tries to control others through coercion, threats, advice giving, helplessness, guilt, manipulation, or domination. Last but not least, he is afraid to let himself be who he really is, and thus often appears rigid and controlled.

Rescuers or co-dependents have very low self-esteem and often feel worthwhile only when they are giving to others, since they get artificial feelings of self-worth from helping others. They create relationships with other people based on the other person's needs and not their own, often enjoying the appearance of being a "savior." Because they don't feel worthy of having love or friendship just because of who they are, they encourage others to be dependent on their ability and willingness to rescue. They constantly try to prove they are good enough for other people, but they settle for being needed. Many co-dependents become professional caretakers, entering such fields as medicine, psychology, counseling, and social work.

Co-dependent relationships are ultimately unhealthy because they inhibit the growth of both parties. The co-dependent cannot become healthy because he is directing his energy and attention away from his own life and issues, and the survivor cannot become healthy because she is prevented from fully experiencing the consequences of her actions and from taking responsibility for her recovery.

Not feeling happy or content with themselves, co-dependents look outside themselves for happiness. They latch onto whomever or whatever they think can provide happiness, desperately searching for love and approval, often from people who are incapable of loving. They worry that people will leave them, and they feel terribly threatened by the loss of anyone or anything they think can provide them with happiness.

Co-dependents have a difficult time asserting their needs, wants, and rights and expressing their emotions openly, honestly, and appropriately, especially the emotions of hurt and anger. They frequently pretend that circumstances are not as bad as they really are. They often repress their anger, and they are afraid of other people's anger. They complain, blame, and try to control, yet they continue to allow others to hurt them. In actuality, co-dependents are a lot more comfortable in complaining and in feeling resentful and bitter than in acknowledging how very hurt and angry they really are.

Certain people are at particularly high risk of becoming co-dependent. These are people who:

- were the children of alcoholic or chemically dependent parents

- ➤ are from a family in which one or both parents were mentally ill or had a long-term serious illness
- ➤ were physically, emotionally, or sexually abused as children
- ➤ are recovering from alcoholism or other chemical dependencies
- ➤ have been married to or have lived with an alcoholic or an addict, especially if there has been more than one such relationship
- ➤ work in the field of mental health, counseling, social work, or chemical-dependency treatment

Asking yourself the following questions can help you to determine whether you are a co-dependent and, if so, to what extent:

---

1. *Do you have a pattern of getting involved with people who have problems and who seem to need you to rescue them?*

2. *Do you spend more time listening to other people's problems than you do talking about or working on your own?*

3. *Do you spend a great deal of time worrying about other people's problems and very little time thinking about your own?*

4. *Do you tend to feel responsible for other people—for their feelings, actions, choices, needs, and well-being?*

5. *Do you feel compelled to help people solve their problems by offering unsolicited advice or by trying to take care of their feelings?*

6. *Do you find it easier to feel and express anger about injustices done to others than about injustices done to you?*

7. *Do you feel safest and most comfortable when you are giving to others?*

8. *Do you feel empty, bored, and worthless if you don't have someone else to take care of, a problem to solve, or a crisis to deal with?*

9. *Do you feel insecure and guilty when someone gives to you?*

10. *Do you stay in relationships that don't work and tolerate abuse in order to keep people loving you?*

If you answered yes to more than half of these questions, you are probably co-dependent. If you suspect that you are co-dependent, you need help. There are Co-dependents Anonymous groups in virtually every city in the United States. In addition, you may want to seek individual therapy in order to work through the guilt, shame, anger, and fear of your own troubled childhood.

SETTING YOUR LIMITS AND ENFORCING YOUR BOUNDARIES

Co-dependent people fail to see the distinctions, or boundaries, between themselves and others. Because they have not taken the time to discover exactly who they are, and because of their excessive need to please others, co-dependents tend to take their identity from, and to merge with, those around them. They let people walk all over them, and then they suddenly get angry because they feel used. One of the things you will need to do in order to recover from co-dependency will be to begin setting personal limits and enforcing your own boundaries.

By no means should you allow yourself to be used, abused, or taken advantage of. Self-care may mean standing up for yourself when your partner starts taking her anger out on you, and perhaps walking away from the situation temporarily if things get too explosive. If the survivor wants more than you are able to give, admit your limits and encourage her to call on other resources. Take some breaks and get help for yourself.

As noted previously, you can't expect yourself to be able to "be there" for your partner or friend at all times. While you may want to be able to listen to her or hold her every single time she needs it, it is not humanly possible for you to do this, and it is certainly not healthy for you to be readily available at all times. There will be times when you are too tired, when you have your own problems, when you are too needy yourself, or when you feel you just can't give anymore. If you do not respect your own limits, you will burn out and will end up resenting all the times you gave when you really didn't want to.

Don't hold back from talking with the survivor about your own needs and problems from time to time, especially when she seems to be going through a less stressful period. While the survivor is the "identified patient," you have your own set of issues to work on, and these are no less important. Whenever your needs cannot be met by the survivor, try to take care of them yourself or with friends, your support group, or a therapist. By all means, avoid getting into an emotional place where you feel so deprived that you become demanding or abusive to the survivor—this is the last thing she or he needs during recovery.

Many co-dependents wait and hope that their partners will *notice* that they need something. This is a real setup for you to feel uncared for. *Tell* your partner what you need; don't expect her to be a mind reader. It is self-defeating to think, "If she loved me enough, she'd know what I want."

Above all, don't fool yourself into thinking that you don't really have needs. We *all* have needs, no matter how strong, self-sufficient, or "together" we are.

You may be a very caring person, capable of great patience and sacrifice—yet everyone has limits. Discovering what yours are and learning to enforce them will be a major part of your own survival during this time.

PART III

Special Issues for Intimate Partners

The information in this section applies to *all* couples dealing with issues of childhood sexual abuse, whether they are married or unmarried, heterosexual, homosexual, or bisexual. While there are, of course, some differences between heterosexual and homosexual couples, these differences are far outweighed by the common problems all couples face when one or both partners are survivors.

Chapter Eight

Dealing with the Sexual Side of Your Relationship

In addition to working with survivors and their partners, I have also worked for many years as a sex therapist. In both capacities I have found that the sexual side of the relationship between a survivor and her partner is by far the most problematic aspect of the relationship. Frequently, while sex may have been great in the beginning of the relationship or before the survivor's sexual abuse issues emerged, it suddenly becomes a problem. Sex becomes a burden for the survivor, a source of rejection for the prosurvivor, and a source of tension for both.

While sex is ideally an expression of love that brings two people closer together, sex between a survivor and her partner is an emotionally loaded experience. Because of her abuse, the survivor may have a distorted and negative view of sex, with anything sexual bringing up feelings of fear, pain, shame, anger, and repulsion in her. Approaching her sexually thus entails some risks. For example, there is a chance that she will accuse you of wanting her only for sex. There is the risk that she will have a flashback and suddenly mistake you for the abuser. There is the risk that something you say will trigger memories for her, or that you will accidentally touch a place on her body that she can't stand having touched. You may try to be tender and gentle, only to have her complain that the passion and fire are no longer there.

You will need to understand how the sexual abuse has affected the survivor's sexuality, what you can do to minimize the amount of trauma she will experience while having sex, and what she must do to heal sexually.

WHAT TO EXPECT

Victims of sexual abuse were either physically forced or emotionally manipulated into a sexual situation with the abuser. If you ever become too forceful, aggressive, or controlling sexually, your lover will feel violated or revictimized. (We will explore this idea further in chapter Ten.) If you coerce or manipulate her into having sex when she really doesn't want it, you are reabusing her. Moreover, if you pressure or threaten her, try to make her feel guilty, or use any other type of manipulation to coerce her into having sex in ways that she does not like, she will also feel revictimized.

When survivors enter therapy, a Twelve-Step program, or any other type of recovery program, memories of the sexual abuse often become much more intense and overwhelming. This is especially true if the survivor is engaged in a sexual relationship. During sex she may begin to have flashbacks during which she suddenly becomes confused about who her partner is. Survivors have been known to actually see the face of the perpetrator as they look at their lover's face.

Your partner may have always had difficulty staying present during sex, but this tendency may increase as recovery progresses. This tendency may become very disconcerting to the prosurvivor. As Gerald told me,

"Jamie will seem to be really enjoying our lovemaking, and then all of a sudden she'll be gone. She grows silent and her body becomes stiff, and I know then that she isn't with me anymore. Fortunately, I've learned to watch for these signals, and I make sure we stop. I don't want to continue when I know she's no longer enjoying it, and even if I did I now understand that it would be damaging to her."

As the survivor becomes more aware of herself and her body, she may need to stop making love as soon as she becomes uncomfortable, stops feeling, or begins to have a flashback.

Some survivors stop having orgasms entirely during parts of the recovery process, while others are able to have them only under certain circumstances.

During sex, both partners tend to be more open and vulnerable, and since the survivor is feeling so much pain in general, it makes sense that some of this pain may spill out whenever she is open. Don't be surprised if your partner begins to cry during sex or afterward. She may be crying because she feels so open and vulnerable, as many women do after sex, or she may be having a flashback. Be aware, too, that orgasms may trigger deep feelings of rage, horror, or sadness for her, and she may cry hard or even hysterically as she climaxes.

When you do engage in sexual activity, go slowly, stopping temporarily whenever necessary. Be willing to shift from a sexual or intimate focus to a loving but nonsexual one if the survivor needs to stop the sexual activity altogether. This will help her begin to trust your intentions and your concern for her.

Avoid using degrading or vulgar terms (such as "fuck," "bitch," "cunt," and "prick"), which can remind survivors of the abuse. Other things to avoid are approaching a survivor from behind, making sudden moves (such as grabbing her quickly), or touching or grabbing her genitals in a teasing manner.

COMMUNICATING OPENLY

Good communication is one of the most important factors in a satisfying sexual relationship. The more you and your partner are able to share with each other your feelings and thoughts about sex, the better your sexual relationship will be.

Learning to communicate openly and honestly needs to become an important part of your sexual relationship with a survivor. While most couples need improvement in this area, survivors and prosurvivors need to work extra hard on learning to ask for what they want and need sexually, and on not assuming they already know what their partner's preferences are. The survivor's needs and preferences can change often during the recovery process, and she may have the tendency to "perform" sexually (doing for you what she thinks you want or what she assumes "all men" like) without really "checking it out." Both of you may have been reticent in the past to talk about sex and to make your preferences known because the issue of sexuality may have become such a sensitive one.

The survivor may have very negative associations with "talking about sex" from her experiences with sexual abuse. The perpetrator may have talked to her during the abuse, using obscene language or telling her how she made him feel. Changing these associations into positive ones will be a challenge, but one which will reap enormous benefits. She may never want to talk during sex, but communicating with you about how she felt following the sexual activity may become a positive experience for her, taking sex out of the abusive, "pornographic" arena, into a more wholesome sharing of intimacy.

While nonverbal communication can sometimes be effective (for example, taking your partner's hand and placing it on the area that you would like to have touched, or moving your partner's hand to show her how you want to be touched), it can also be easily misunderstood or misinterpreted. A survivor may be reminded of the way the perpetrator took her hand and placed it on his penis or she may comply to your nonverbal signals but experience them as a demand.

The idea that we can tell our partner what we want by doing it to them can also backfire, as was the case with Gaby and Wade. Gaby loved to have her legs stroked and tried to communicate this to her boyfriend, Wade, by stroking his legs. Unfortunately, Wade didn't seem to get the message, and seldom if ever touched her legs. After they began to communicate more openly with each other, Wade shared with Gaby that he didn't like to have his legs touched. Gaby was shocked to realize that not only had she been unsuccessful in communicating to Wade what she wanted, but he had been putting up with her touches all that time.

Both you and your partner may initially feel too vulnerable or too fearful of rejection or ridicule to talk openly with each other. It will take time to build a feeling of safety between you in which you can risk talking about your most intimate feelings.

During this time of change and reevaluation, be as open and honest as you can about your own feelings, and ask your partner questions to find out how she is feeling. You don't necessarily have to have an open dialogue during sex, although many survivors and their partners find this to be very helpful. Don't let too much time elapse between conversations, especially if you are confused or unclear about something. For example, if your partner seemed to become numb during sex, ask her what just happened. If she doesn't want to talk about it at the moment, wait until it seems like a good time to talk and gently ask her again. Do not barrage her with questions; simply tell her you want to know what happened so that you can learn from it. If she still isn't ready to talk, give her some time. She may need time alone to understand what really did happen, or she may need to talk to her therapist or group first.

As mentioned, survivors frequently confuse their partners with their abusers. Certain things that you say or do, particularly when you show affection or when the two of you are making love, can remind your partner of the perpetrator and cause her to see you as the abuser. Unless your partner feels free to tell you when you have done or said something that has triggered a memory for her, you may never know what buttons you have inadvertently pushed. Ask her to tell you the kinds of things that the perpetrator said and did so that you will have a better idea of what to avoid. You can't expect to totally avoid triggering bad memories for her, of course, but if you at least know some of the things that might upset her ahead of time you have a better chance of avoiding some upsets. For example, even your saying "I love you" may send a survivor into a tailspin, since the perpetrator may have said the same thing.

If during sex you begin to feel that your partner is relating not to you but rather to the abuser, stop whatever you are doing and check it out. A simple question such as "Are you all right?" or "What's going on?" can sometimes bring a survivor back to the present. Other times you may need to be more specific, asking, for example, "Are you remembering something?" or "Are you having a flashback?" By talking and working together when negative feelings surface, you and your partner can overcome many of the problems of dissociation and flashbacks.

LETTING HER MAKE THE RULES

In order for a survivor to heal sexually, she must not do anything she doesn't genuinely want to do. This will likely be very difficult for her, because she is used to having sex even when she doesn't feel like it. In addition to damaging her in numerous ways, the sexual abuse taught her to be submissive and compliant and to split off from herself when things become uncomfortable, unpleasant, or painful. For example, while the average person (particularly a woman) may find it somewhat difficult to assert herself and say no to someone initiating sex when she does not want it, a survivor will also have difficulty saying no to sex that is repulsive to her or that causes her great emotional or even physical pain. Instead, she will "go away" in her mind by focusing on something else or finding some other way of splitting off from herself and how she is feeling. All the while, her body is lying there, engaged in an act that is traumatizing her.

Your responsibility will be to always ask your partner whether or not she wants to be sexual at any given time, and whether she is sure if she wants to engage in any particular type of sexual activity. You will both need to take a lot of time with your sexual relationship, reexamining every aspect of it, including how often you have sex, when you have sex (what time of day, whether it's okay with her to have sex when the children are at home, whether it's okay to have sex on the day she's had her therapy session), what kind of sex you have (fondling, intercourse, oral sex, anal sex), and where you have sex.

This reevaluation will most likely have a radical effect on your sexual relationship. Many survivors want to engage only in sexual activities that were not a part of the sexual abuse. The survivor may want sex only under very controlled circumstances. She may want you to touch her only in certain places. Or, she may want only to touch you, with you not touching her at all. She may need a lot more foreplay than she had previously led you to believe, or she may not want any foreplay at all. She may need to be massaged or caressed before or after sex. She may want to be held afterward. She may want sex only when there will be time to talk before or after sex, and so on.

For example, if the perpetrator fondled her but did not engage in intercourse, the survivor may not want to engage in any kind of foreplay at all before intercourse. If the opposite was true—that is, if she was penetrated without any foreplay—she may only want to be fondled, caressed, and brought to orgasm manually or orally. If the perpetrator did everything to her but intercourse, intercourse may be the only thing she can do that is free of any association or memory of the abuser and free of any trauma. If the perpetrator did everything but engage in oral sex, that may be the one expression of sexuality that is truly enjoyable to her.

The same can hold true of which parts of her body she wants to have touched and which parts of your body she is willing to touch. If the perpetrator fondled her nipples she may not want you touching them at all. If he touched her everywhere except her nipples it may be extremely pleasurable and erotic to her to have you touch or kiss them since they have no negative associations.

For many survivors, it becomes important to be the initiator of sex, at least for some time during recovery. This simple decision can change a lot about how the survivor feels about sex. No longer having to worry about responding to your overtures, she may be able to relax and feel her sexuality a lot more freely than ever before. Initiating sex also provides the survivor with a sense of being in control—something she may never have had before regarding sex. This doesn't mean that you have to give up all control in all aspects of your relationship, or even in terms of your sexuality, for that matter. It just means that you let her make all sexual overtures. Many prosurvivor partners have actually welcomed this change, especially if they have felt that they always had to make the first move.

Dale was pleased with the change this decision made in his relationship with his wife:

"One of the best things we ever did was to make the rule that she would always be the initiator. I was tired of always being the one to ask for sex. It always put me in the position of being the one who was rejected, and it felt terrible. But now I just wait for her, and I've been surprised to find out that she wants sex more than I had ever thought she would! She's been pleasantly surprised, too, to realize that without the pressure of worrying about when I was going to ask for sex, she was free to discover her own sexual needs."

Intimate partners often fear that if they stop initiating sex, they will never get any. This certainly is a real concern, considering the situation. However, because the survivor is not begin pressured to engage in sexual activity, she may be able to begin to trust that you want to be with her for reasons other than sexual contact. This was the case with Cindy:

"When my boyfriend stopped pressuring me for sex and even seemed okay with the fact that I didn't initiate it either for a while, I suddenly began to believe that he really loved me. I thought, 'Here's this guy who could be with other women if he wanted to, and he isn't even getting sex from me, but he's still *with* me. I guess he must really love me.' After that, I found that I did want to have sex sometimes, just because I wanted to be close to him and feel that connection."

TAKING TIME OUT FROM SEX

Sometimes, the survivor realizes that she doesn't want to have sex at all for a while. This doesn't mean that things are going wrong, but that a period of celibacy is what's called for. Although these times are likely to be difficult for the prosurvivor, it may be essential to the survivor. For many survivors, taking time out from sex—whether for six days or six months—can be a healing in itself, providing them with the time and space to free themselves of negative associations with sex and helping them to come back to sex with an entirely different outlook.

The time-out from sex can be just as beneficial for the prosurvivor and for the relationship as it is for the survivor herself. Many of us have grown so accustomed to getting all of our intimacy needs met through sexual activity that we are unable to feel and express intimacy in any other way. There are many other ways of sharing intimacy—for example, holding hands, caressing and massaging, taking a bath or Jacuzzi together, cuddling, rubbing each other's backs, or just taking a walk together. The time-out from sex can encourage you and your partner to develop mutually pleasurable, nonsexual experiences of touch and intimacy. (Later on in this chapter, I will guide you through several sensate-focus exercises to help you with these alternatives.) Also, as a result of exploring a variety of ways of expressing intimacy, you will likely become far less compulsive and goal-oriented than you may now be when it comes to sex.

HOW TO HANDLE FEELINGS OF REJECTION

It is common for intimate partners to feel rejected and angry because of all the changes in their sexual relationship. Even though you understand that your partner needs to be able to decide for herself when she does and doesn't want to have sex, the rejection you feel may be profound, as Herbert discovered:

"Ramona had always been willing to have sex with me whenever I approached her. It was quite a shock to discover, after 13 years of marriage, that a great deal of the time she had just been doing it to please me! While I encouraged her to make sure she had sex with me only when she really wanted to, the first time she said no came as a terrible rejection to me. I tried to reason with myself and talk myself out of feeling rejected, but I just couldn't. I felt hurt, and that's all there was to it. Fortunately, we were able to talk about it, and Ramona was able to assure me that she loved me."

Sometimes, words of reassurance are all that you will need. If your partner can tell you that she loves you and that she wants to be with you, your hurt feelings may subside rather quickly. On the other hand, sometimes words alone won't do it. You may need to be *physically* reassured as well.

Dylan, a young client of mine in his early twenties, told me:

"I soon discovered that I needed some physical connection with my girlfriend, even if it wasn't sexual. I could take her saying no if she reassured me with a touch or by holding me. She tried it and discovered that it helped her, too, because it reassured her that I still loved *her* even though she had said no. Now, if she isn't in the place to have sex, we spend lots of time cuddling, rubbing each other's backs, or just lying close together."

Some people have such a difficult time with rejection that they become withdrawn and hesitate to reach out to their partners again. This was the case with Lee, who was in a lesbian relationship with Jennifer:

"The first time Jennifer said no to me, I felt like someone had hit me in the stomach. I was so devastated that I just lay back and became kind of paralyzed. I tried to make sense of it in my mind, telling myself that I was okay and that Jennifer still loved me, but I didn't *feel* okay—I felt utterly abandoned. She saw how I was reacting and tried to comfort me, but her words couldn't reach me. It was like I had gone far, far away from her."

Because Lee's mother had physically abandoned her when she was only two years old, leaving her in a foster home where she got very little affection, Lee had a high degree of sensitivity to any kind of rejection. Through therapy, Lee was able to understand this and to work through much of her pain about her mother's rejection of her so that she did not continue to relive it in her relationship with Jennifer.

If you find that you are unable to "bounce back" when you have felt rejected or if you experience feelings of intense pain whenever you are rejected, you may need to work with a therapist on your rejection issues from your past.

Many prosurvivors begin to feel undesirable and/or inadequate sexually. Following are some of the commonly heard complaints of partners of survivors:

- "I feel unattractive and unloved."
- "I haven't felt free to express my sexual desires because of what it does to her, and as a result I don't *feel* very sexual anymore."
- "I try to understand that she just needs a time-out from sex, but I can't help thinking that if I were a better lover she would want sex with me more often."

Some male partners begin to experience problems with achieving and maintaining an erection or with ejaculation (either ejaculating prematurely or having difficulty ejaculating at all). Other partners become overwhelmed with the loneliness and pain caused by the emotional distance they feel from the survivor often without the survivor's even being aware of it. Problems such as lack of sexual desire and lack of sexual confidence may result and may become as difficult a problem in the relationship as the problems suffered by the survivor.

It is vitally important that you understand that the survivor's difficulties with sex stem from the sexual abuse *and are not a reflection of her feelings toward you*. Keep in mind the reasons why a survivor has difficulty with sexuality and trust. Instead of either pressuring her or withdrawing, work to keep the lines of communication open, telling her your feelings and eliciting hers. State your needs in as clear and nonpressuring a manner as possible. Instead of saying, for example, "We haven't had sex in three weeks. How long is this going to go on?," try expressing not only your sexual needs but your desire for intimacy and closeness—something like, "I love you. Sex is important to me; it is one of the ways I can express loving feelings for you and have you express yours to me. But I don't want to pressure you into having sex unless you feel like it. Maybe we could just hold each other and give each other a massage, so that I can get some reassurance and affection and can have a way to let you know I love you."

SENSATE-FOCUS EXERCISES

The following exercises originated with the work of sex therapists Masters and Johnson. In my practice, these exercises have helped hundreds of couples suffering from a vast variety of sexual and intimacy problems. They are designed to help establish trust between partners and to help them find alternative ways of touching and sharing intimacy. "Sensate-focus" refers to the fact that during the exercises you are to *focus* your attention as closely as you can on your *sensations*—that is, on how it feels to touch or be touched.

It has been proved that this particular way of touching, called caressing, removes the pressure to perform, allows each person to touch for his or her own pleasure, and helps each partner to express tenderness, caring, and gentleness.

Caressing is different from massage or even from what is commonly called "sensual" massage in that instead of manipulating the large muscles of the body, you focus on the skin. Caressing is a slow, sensuous touch that is much lighter than massage and is done very, very slowly, using not just the tips of the fingers but the entire hand and even the forearm.

Another difference between caressing and massaging is that while massage is intended solely for the pleasure or therapeutic benefit of the person *receiving* the massage, caressing is done for the pleasure of the person *giving* the caress as well. You may have noticed in the past that you became tired easily while giving a massage, and you may even have become anxious because you were concerned about whether you were doing it correctly and pleasing the person you were massaging. In caressing, the person doing the giving enjoys the activity as much as the person on the receiving end. Caressing is thus a shared pleasure, not a task.

To understand exactly what I mean, try the following exercise:

Imagine that your right hand is the "giver" and your left hand is the "receiver." Touch your left hand using only the fingertips of your right hand. Which of your hands feels the pleasure of the touch? Most people will say that their left hand, the "receiver," feels the pleasure. But what about your right hand? Most people say they do not feel any pleasure in that hand.

Now, however, try touching your left hand by using the flat of the palm, fingers, and wrist of your right hand. Which hand feels the pleasure of the touch this time? Most people say that *both* hands feel it. Indeed, it is hard to tell which hand is the giver and which the receiver.

You and your partner may or may not choose to use a lotion or oil for the caressing. Some people do not like the feel of lotion or oil on their skin, and some survivors may have a negative association with lotion or oil, especially if the perpetrator used it. If you do decide to use one, make sure it's one that you both like. Also, make certain the fragrance does not elicit any negative memories for either one of you.

Always do the exercises in a private, quiet environment. Take the phone off the hook and send the children to a baby-sitter or wait until they are in bed at night. While some people prefer to have some relaxing music on, it is really best to do these exercises in silence, since it's too easy to become distracted when there is music. The important thing here is to focus on sensations only.

Whether you are the one who is giving the touch or receiving it, make sure that you always focus all your attention on the point where your body comes in contact with your partner's skin. If your mind wanders off during the exercise, bring it back to the exact point between your skin and your partner's skin.

When You Are the Active Partner

Do not speak while doing the exercise, and do not ask for feedback. *Do not worry about whether your partner is enjoying the caress.* It will be her responsibility to let you know if you are doing something that feels uncomfortable to her. If possible, do the exercise with your eyes closed most of the time.

Always maintain contact with your partner as you are giving the caress to avoid surprising her with a sudden touch when you switch hands. If you use lotion or oil, warm it in your hand before you apply it, and maintain contact with your partner's body when you reapply it.

You can use long, sweeping strokes, using your forearm, wrist, the palm of your hand, and the flat of your fingers, or you can alternate with shorter strokes, using only the flat of your fingers. Make sure that you do not use your fingertips, however, because this can tickle your partner.

Make sure that your motions are very, very slow—the slower the better. If you think you are moving your hand slowly enough, cut your speed in half and see how this affects your ability to focus on the touch.

While you will be focusing mostly on your own feelings while caressing your partner, you should be able to notice whether she seems anxious or tense. Obvious signs of anxiety include rapid or shallow breathing, a jumpy or quivering stomach, and muscle tension.

If you notice any of these signs in your partner, slow your touch down. If signs of anxiety do not go away, encourage your partner to take deep breaths. If she still seems tense, ask her if she'd like to stop the exercise for a while until she becomes more comfortable.

When You Are the Passive Partner

Close your eyes and try to relax any muscles that feel tense. Keep your attention on the place where your partner is touching your skin. Mentally follow your partner's hand as it caresses your body. Do not give your partner any feedback unless something is painful or uncomfortable. Do not moan or groan or wiggle around. This can be threatening to a survivor because it may sound to her as though you are becoming sexually aroused. It can also be a way of manipulating the active partner into continuing to touch a particular spot. By remaining completely passive, you will allow your body to experience pleasure more fully. If you become tense, try taking some deep breaths to relax yourself and focus only on the touch.

Feedback

Once each sensate-focus exercise is over, it is important for you and your partner to give each other feedback on what you experienced during the exercise. Talk openly and honestly with each other about your experience. Most people benefit greatly from this feedback, which can be the beginning of honest communication between two partners establishing trust and openness. The exercises will not be as beneficial if you are not honest about your feelings. For instance, do not tell your partner you enjoyed the experience if you didn't, or that you were able to concentrate if you weren't, just so you will appear to be doing things correctly.

While your first attempts at giving feedback may seem awkward, after a few times it will become much easier and feel more natural. Use the following questions as guidelines to facilitate your feedback:

When you were in the passive role, were you able to relax completely and accept the pleasure for yourself, or did you feel pressured to respond and express to your partner how great it was?

While in the active role, were you able to focus on your own pleasure rather than worrying about whether your partner was enjoying the caress? Did you feel pressured to perform, or did you touch her the way you wanted to?

Which role were you most comfortable with, the active or the passive role? Was it easier for you to focus in one role more than in the other?

Did you feel anxious during the exercise? Were you able to calm yourself by focusing, deep breathing, and relaxing? Did you become less anxious as the exercise progressed or more anxious?

Did you enjoy the caress? What part of the caress did you enjoy the most? What part of your partner's body did you enjoy touching the most? What part of your body did you enjoy having touched the most?

Was it easy for you to stay within the limits of the exercise, or did you want to touch areas outside the bounds of the exercise?

The Exercises

The following exercises should bring you much closer together than you have ever been before, and they will add to your repertoire of sensual ways of sharing.

Foot Caress

If at all possible, keep your eyes closed during most of this exercise, even when you are in the active role. You may do this exercise either with or without a foot bath. The foot bath can be a loving, relaxing part of this exercise and should be included if at all possible. (It also solves any problem of foot odor.) If you leave out the bath, all you need is some oil or lotion and two towels. If you include the foot bath, you will need two towels, liquid soap, lotion, warm water, and a basin or tub large enough for a person's feet.

To start, the passive person sits in a chair with his or her feet on the floor. Since this exercise includes the ankles and part of the calves, the partner who will receive the massage needs to have his or her pant legs rolled up or wear shorts. The active partner fills the basin with warm water and places the passive partner's feet in the water. Add the liquid soap and slowly bathe and caress one foot at a time, remembering to use a light touch, not a massage. Touch for your own pleasure, discovering how the different areas of the feet feel to you as you bathe them. Spend at least five minutes on each foot, and longer if you like.

When you are finished with both feet, lift them out of the water one at a time, dry them, and wrap them in separate towels. Put the basin aside. Now gently take one foot from its towel and caress it, using the oil or lotion. Take as long as you like, staying longer on the parts of the foot, ankle, and lower calf that you especially enjoy touching. Spend at least five to ten minutes on each foot.

When you are the passive person, all you have to do is relax and enjoy, allowing yourself to be pampered. If your partner does something that bothers you, say something, but otherwise concentrate totally on the touch. Relax your feet and just let them hang from your legs. Your partner will lift them into the basin and move them—you don't need to help.

Back Caress

The back caress may be more threatening to the survivor than the hand or foot caress, since it can involve parts of the body that are often associated with sexual arousal, such as the buttocks and thighs. You and your partner need to agree in advance that there will be no sexual touching, and that you will confine your touching to areas of the body that are "in bounds." While the back caress will actually include the entire back of the body, from the neck to the feet, you may want to confine yourselves to the upper back, above the waist only.

This exercise can be done in the nude. However, since many survivors may still be uncomfortable with nudity at this point, I recommend that you both wear shorts, bathing suits, or underwear. Women may feel comfortable in a halter top or a bra.

As always, you will need a quiet room where you will not be disturbed, with a bed or some other comfortable surface with plenty of room for both of you to stretch out. You will also need a large towel and some lotion or oil.

The passive partner should lie comfortably, face down, on the towel. She may place her arms at her sides or beneath her head, whichever is more comfortable. Either lie down on your side next to the passive partner, but without leaning on her or sit next to her, whichever is more comfortable for you. Both of you should have your eyes closed when at all possible in order to enhance the pleasure and maximize your ability to focus.

Begin to caress your partner's back with one hand, beginning at the neck. Slowly and lightly run your palm or fingers over her shoulder blades, then down her spine.

If the two of you have agreed to include the entire back of the body, continue touching your partner, moving down the back to the buttocks and legs. If you have difficulty focusing on the physical sensations, slow your speed down and bring your mind back to the exact point of contact between your skin and your partner's.

Pay attention to how the various parts of your partner's body feel when you caress them with your palm, wrist, and forearm instead of just your fingertips. When you find that a particular part of the body feels especially good to you, savor the touch and languish there a while. Pay attention to the various textures of the skin and the different temperatures of various parts of the body.

Again, *there should be no sexual touching with this exercise*. Do not include the genitals, and do not place your hands inside the crevice of the buttocks. The survivor must be able to feel completely safe knowing that you are not going to go beyond the limits of the exercise.

If you notice that your partner is tensing up, remind her to breathe and relax, and continue with the caress. If, after a few minutes, she still seems tense and is moving about or breathing rapidly, stop the caress and talk quietly about this before either continuing the exercise or suspending it for the time being.

Spend approximately 20 to 30 minutes doing the back caress. Complete it with long, smooth strokes, starting at your partner's shoulders and moving all the way down to her feet. You may want to indicate that you have stopped by placing your hands firmly on the bottoms of her feet.

When you are the passive partner, make yourself comfortable, breathe deeply, and relax your muscles. Keep your mind on the exact point where your partner is touching you. Try not to move; just passively soak up the sensations. As always in these exercises, communicate with your partner only if something feels uncomfortable to you.

If you become sexually aroused either as the giver or the receiver during the back caress, fine. Just enjoy the arousal and bring your mind back to the point of contact.

Summary of things to remember for doing sensate-focus exercises:

1. *Agree on the limits of the exercise beforehand and do not go beyond those limits.*

2. *Always focus on the point of contact where your skin touches your partner's skin.*

3. *When you are the active partner, do the exercise for your own pleasure, and do not worry whether your partner is enjoying it. Use a slow, light, caressing technique.*

4. *Stay passive when in the passive role—unless something feels uncomfortable, give no feedback.*

5. *Focus on sensual pleasure, not on sexual arousal.*

6. *If anxiety does not quickly decrease after the first few minutes of an exercise, stop the exercise immediately.*

7. *Don't work at it—relax!*

8. *Provide honest feedback to each other after the exercise.*

THAT'S FINE MOST OF THE TIME, BUT . . .

There will be times when no amount of reassurance and no amount of touching are going to take the place of making love. The deep longing for this will sometimes surface, and as hard as you try, as patient as you are, there will be times when you will just feel deprived, frustrated, and angry. These feelings are natural; let yourself feel them, instead of trying to bury them in your attempts to be understanding and patient. As long as you aren't abusive in doing so, share your feelings with your partner. She needs to know that at times you are angry, and talking it over with her will help clear the air. This was the case with Van and his wife:

"I finally told Lindsey how hopeless I sometimes feel, and how afraid I am that she will never really get any better and that we will always have a sexless marriage. I told her how tired I am of going to bed night after night wanting sex but knowing I'm not going to get it. Much to my surprise, she didn't seem to get all that upset. She seemed to really understand. She told me she didn't blame me for getting angry and impatient sometimes, that I wouldn't be human if I didn't. She said it made her trust me more for me to tell her the truth about how I really feel, since she knew I couldn't possibly be as understanding as I sometimes pretend to be. I really felt better after our talk, and so did she."

There are, of course, some things you will not want to share with your partner because they would be just too painful for her. After Barry had been married to Crystal for two years, he discovered that she had been sexually abused by her father. Although she and Barry had been having sex regularly, Crystal decided rather suddenly that she no longer wanted to engage in any sexual activity at all. Barry tried to be understanding and to find alternative ways of sharing intimacy, but sometimes he just became so frustrated and angry that he had to let off steam. As he told me during one of our sessions:

"Sometimes I just feel like going out and having an affair. After all, I don't know how long this ban on sex is going to go on. There are lots of women at work who come on to me. Why shouldn't I get what I need? Crystal would never need to find out, and I could relieve some of my frustration. I'm not a saint, you know. I love Crystal, but I have my own needs. So far, all we've done is take care of *her* needs."

Barry didn't have an affair, and I didn't really think he would. He just needed a place to complain and to release some of his anger and frustration.

To summarize: By doing the following, you will help build the atmosphere of trust and safety necessary for the survivor to work through her sexual problems and to begin to view sex in an entirely different way:

---

1. *Encourage your partner to say no at any time and to have sex only when she really wants to.*

2. *Discuss your sexual concerns openly and honestly with your partner, and communicate your feelings without blaming her.*

3. *Don't pressure your partner for sex or try to manipulate her into doing things she doesn't want to do.*

4. *Find ways of sharing intimacy that are nonsexual, such as cuddling, massaging, and caressing.*

5. *Negotiate compromises with your partner that take into consideration both of your needs.*

6. *Approach sexual activity in a patient, relaxed manner, emphasizing fun and intimacy instead of performance and goals.*

7. *Accept the fact that both you and your partner may experience different levels of sexual desire at different times.*

Through patience, commitment, good communication, and caring, you and your partner can weather the recovery process and establish a fulfilling and healthy sexual relationship. The next chapter will deal with the kinds of specific sexual dysfunctions that plague survivors of childhood sexual abuse. There is also a general discussion of sexual dysfunctions, including those you may suffer from.

Chapter Nine

The Special Problem of Sexual Dysfunction

I started out working as a sex therapist long before I became a licensed psychotherapist, partly as a way of discovering what was wrong with myself sexually. As a young woman, I was unable to reach orgasm or to relax and enjoy myself sexually. Sex was always a performance, mostly intended to please the man. I did not share my inability with my partners but instead faked orgasm.

While I want to share my expertise as a sex therapist with you, I don't want to scare you off with too much "technical" information. However, in the interest of accuracy, and so that you can do further reading if you are interested, I will use terms that are commonly used among professionals.

When I began working as a sex therapist I discovered that many of the people I was working with had themselves been sexually abused as children, and that this trauma had caused their sexual dysfunctions.

Many survivors of sexual abuse do, indeed, suffer from a number of sexual dysfunctions. Even though a survivor may feel ready to engage in sexual activity again, she may need to work on a specific sexual dysfunction. This can be done with the assistance of a certified sex therapist, or the survivor may discover her sexual dysfunction is eliminated as she continues in the healing process.

FEMALE SEXUAL DYSFUNCTION

Female Sexual Arousal Disorder

This disorder, which is the most common dysfunction for women survivors, is the inability to become sexually aroused. This may involve failure to lubricate or a lack of sexual excitement or pleasure. The survivor may be often reminded of the abuse during sex, or she may be traumatized by any sexual contact. During the recovery process, female survivors often suffer from this dysfunction for long periods of time, finding relief only as they experience more and more healing and can begin to separate the present from the past.

Vaginismus

Another common dysfunction for female survivors is vaginismus, an involuntary contracting or tightening of the vaginal muscles, particularly those around the opening of the vagina. Vaginismus can cause intercourse to be uncomfortable, painful, or even impossible. It is sometimes accompanied by muscle tightness in the stomach, thighs, and buttocks. For women who were raped, either as children or as adults, and for those who were molested by having fingers and instruments inserted into their vaginas, vaginismus is often a defense against pain.

There are different degrees of vaginismus. Some women experience it only in response to attempts at insertion of the penis, while others may not be able to insert anything into the vagina, not even a finger or a tampon. It is also possible that vaginismus can occur with one partner and not with others.

Many women have vaginismus without realizing it. Instead, a survivor and her partner may think that the partner's penis is exceptionally large, or that the woman's vagina is unusually small or tight. However, vaginismus is not related to the size of the man's penis or the woman's vagina. When properly lubricated and stimulated, the female vagina can comfortably accommodate any penis size. It is extremely rare for a vagina to be so small that it will not accommodate even a very small penis.

Many survivors encounter the problem of vaginismus the first time they voluntarily choose to have sex, but gradually get over it as they have more and more experience with sex that isn't abusive or violent. Others will periodically suffer from the problem whenever they are reminded of the abuse. Still others will need to wait until they have completed more of their recovery before they will be relieved of this problem. Sally's husband, Kenneth, recalled:

"The first time I tried to penetrate my wife she was so closed up that I couldn't get inside her. I didn't know what was wrong, but I took it personally. I thought I must not be spending enough time with foreplay. But no matter how long I spent, she was never really ready. Finally, we went to a doctor who told us what was wrong. That's when it came out that Sally had been raped by her stepfather, and that's when she started therapy.

"It took her a long time before she was finally able to have intercourse with me. Fortunately, we learned to do a lot of other things instead. Even today I still have to be very gentle and move very slowly, or she'll tense up. And sometimes, if she's been talking about the rape with her therapist recently and reexperiencing the feelings she had, she'll tighten up completely again and we won't be able to have intercourse for a few weeks."

Learning to relax is the most important factor in overcoming vaginismus. Any of the caressing exercises described earlier can help in this. Then, when the survivor begins to feel more relaxed, she can begin to work on the problem by inserting her own fingers into her vagina. When she feels even more comfortable, she and her partner can work on it together: she should first insert her partner's fingers into her vagina, then his penis. Note that it is she who should control all insertion.

MALE SEXUAL DYSFUNCTION

Erectile Disorders

Male survivors frequently suffer from problems with erection, referred to by professionals either as male erectile disorder or as impotence (though this is now considered an older term).

Some male survivors have erections through masturbation but never with a partner. Some have had erections in the past, but at some point have become unable to have them. Still others can have erections but are unable to have them consistently with their partners. Others are consistently able to achieve erections but lose them during lovemaking and before ejaculation.

The most common reason for erectile disorders is that the survivors' self-esteem and self-confidence were so damaged by the sexual abuse that they literally feel impotent, or powerless, in life. Common synonyms for the word *impotent* are, in fact, "powerless," "ineffective," "helpless," "weak," and "disabled."

Another common reason for such disorders is that the erect male penis symbolizes power and aggressiveness, and many male survivors do not want to be identified with these things. To many male survivors, the erect penis also represents violence, intrusiveness, and pain. The survivor's own penis may remind him of his violation, as in Patrick's case:

"Almost every time I see my own erection, I see the erect penis of my perpetrator. It makes me feel nauseous, afraid, and angry all at the same time. Within seconds I have lost my own erection and I am that eight-year-old boy once again, being forced to touch and suck a male's erect penis."

Some men, aware of the potential violence brewing inside them, may unconsciously choose to be impotent rather than risk the possibility that their rage could erupt and cause them to rape women or children. Frank, one of my clients, had suffered for 10 years with the inability to achieve an erection while with a woman. In therapy, he finally got to the root of his problem.

Frank's mother, an alcoholic, had been very sexually seductive with him from the time he was two or three years old. By the time he was nine or ten his mother was stimulating his penis to erection, and finally to ejaculation. It wasn't until one day when he was sixteen that Frank was finally able to call a halt to the abuse, but only by pushing his mother away with such force that she was knocked unconscious against a wall. Experiencing what he was capable of when he was angry, coupled with having frequent rape fantasies, frightened Frank so much that it had rendered him impotent. Once Frank was able to make the connection between his impotence and his rage toward his mother, he was able to begin the recovery process, which included finding constructive ways of releasing years and years of pent-up anger.

Premature Ejaculation

Another common sexual dysfunction among male survivors is premature, or rapid, ejaculation. This problem is defined not by the amount of time or the number of thrusts before ejaculation, but by the man's feeling of not being in control over when he ejaculates. Survivors who suffer from this disorder experience it in varying degrees. Some ejaculate with no physical or sexual stimulation at all, some when they are rubbed up against, some as soon as they are touched by a hand or mouth, and some immediately upon penetration or only a few seconds afterward.

A major cause of premature ejaculation is anxiety. Since survivors tend to experience a tremendous amount of anxiety when they become sexually involved, it only stands to reason that this could, indeed, cause prematurity. Some men are not aware of how very anxious they are, while others may be acutely aware of feeling panicky at the very thought of a sexual encounter. Either way, their bodies have learned a response in which their tensed muscles, irregular breathing patterns, and distracting thoughts are triggering early ejaculation.

Many survivors are premature ejaculators because they literally want to get the sex act over with. Rick was one of many of my male clients who expressed this sentiment in one way or another:

"I was always so tense and fearful during sex that I just wanted to ejaculate and get it all over with. Even though I sometimes felt guilty because I knew the woman wasn't satisfied, I mostly just felt relieved."

My client Carlos was able to understand what his anxiety was all about:

"When I was a little boy, there was a group of boys who taunted me all the time. They made fun of how I dressed, where I lived, and even the way I talked. Every day after school they would be waiting for me, and they would yell things at me all the way home. One day, they all circled around me and started taking off my pants, laughing at my embarrassment as I stood there naked. Then they all started laughing at my penis and saying how little and ugly it was. All of a sudden, I ejaculated! I had never been so humiliated in my life. They all laughed hysterically and started calling me a queer. From that day on, I had the label of 'queer' in school. It followed me into high school, where I was terrified of gym class because I was afraid I would ejaculate whenever I took off my clothes or took a shower, and the other guys would think I was turned on by them. To my horror I did ejaculate several times, but fortunately no one ever saw me.

"I grew up convinced that I was gay and that I had an ugly penis. I didn't get involved with a woman until I was 25, and then I was always premature. All a woman had to do was look at me and I ejaculated."

By learning to recognize their levels of anxiety (and what the anxiety specifically relates to) and their levels of arousal, survivors who experience this type of dysfunction can learn to last as long as they want to.

PROBLEMS FOR BOTH SEXES

The Inability to Have an Orgasm

One of the most common sexual dysfunctions for both male and female survivors is the inability to have an orgasm. In females this is called "inhibited female orgasm" (in the past it was referred to as "inorgasmia," "anorgasmia," "preorgasmia," or "frigidity"). In males the problem is called "inhibited ejaculation," "retarded ejaculation," or "ejaculatory incompetence."

Some survivors are unable to climax in any way, while others are able to climax while masturbating but not during intercourse or other types of lovemaking. Some can only reach a climax when they are in control of the sexual act, such as being on top, being the initiator, or being the one who is doing the moving.

The reasons for difficulty in achieving orgasm are varied, but the issue of control is always at the core of the problem. When a child is sexually violated, that child loses all sense of control over his or her body. Holding back from having an orgasm, even though it is an unconscious act, is one way of asserting control over one's body.

As mentioned earlier in the book, because the survivor's trust was violated by the sexual abuse, as an adult she finds it difficult to trust others. To have an orgasm with her partner, she must be able to feel comfortable, trusting, and vulnerable. Without trust, there is no true vulnerability. The survivor's fear of being betrayed, hurt, used, and then discarded may keep her from relaxing enough to be truly vulnerable with you. She may be afraid of feeling pleasure for fear that you will take advantage of her, as the perpetrator did, or she may be afraid of loving you for fear that you are just using her, as the perpetrator did.

Some victims had an orgasm while they were being violated. It gave them a feeling of terrible humiliation to realize that their bodies could be manipulated into doing something against their will. Many survivors have talked about feeling as if their bodies have betrayed them because they felt pleasure or climaxed even though they were being violated and didn't *want* to feel any pleasure. Because of this kind of experience, some survivors closed themselves off from feeling sexual pleasure. They vowed to never again allow themselves to feel that their bodies were out of control. Even those who felt no sexual pleasure during the abuse may have secretly vowed to themselves that they would always maintain control over their own bodies.

Some survivors are able to have orgasms only while lost in a fantasy, because feeling connected to their partners or becoming too intimate may be far too threatening. Unfortunately, these fantasies may sometimes be unhealthy ones, such as those of being forced to have sex, being overpowered by strangers, or even of being with the perpetrator. While this may seem very sick to you and may make you wonder whether this means the survivor actually *enjoyed* being abused, this is absolutely not the case: no victim of sexual abuse enjoyed being violated, betrayed, damaged, manipulated, or controlled. What is occurring is an arousal factor based on the body's having responded to the stimuli during the abuse.

This is particularly true if the sexual abuse was the victim's first sexual experience. Our first experience with sex is highly charged and is therefore intensely erotic and strongly remembered. Even though the victim was forced to do things against her will, there may have been erotic elements present, such as the feeling of physical pleasure or the experience of having the perpetrator express sexual pleasure. These memories stay locked in the mind and body long after the abuse, and they can cause the survivor to become aroused even while feeling a great deal of shame about the arousal.

If the only way a survivor can have an orgasm is to replay the abuse in her mind, she may opt to do this, either because she wants to relieve the sexual tension she has built up or to please her partner. The survivor is thus out of control and is in a real sense being revictimized by her own erotic fantasies. Not only is she reexperiencing the trauma of her childhood each time she uses such a fantasy to bring her to orgasm, but she is damaging her already low self-esteem by doing something she is ashamed of. She may think that she is crazy or that she must have encouraged the perpetrator. Thus, a vicious circle is perpetuated: the more she uses these forbidden fantasies, the worse she feels about herself; the worse she feels about herself, the less likely she will be to become able to get close to someone else.

A survivor need not have a sexual fantasy that is a replay of the actual abuse (in which she would imagine her perpetrator having sex with her, for example) for her fantasies to be damaging to her. Any sexual fantasy in which she is being forced, dominated, overpowered, humiliated, or hurt by anyone, is likely to be a consequence of the sexual abuse and thus, in essence, is a replaying of the experience.

As I have already mentioned many times, victims of sexual abuse suffer from very low self-esteem, which can make them feel unlovable, unattractive, and undesirable as a sexual partner. The survivor may thus have a difficult time relaxing during sex and may instead be preoccupied wondering whether or not you find her attractive, whether you are being critical of her, and whether she is responding correctly. The more you can reassure your partner that you find her attractive and are not being critical or impatient with her, the more relaxed she will become.

It is very important that partners do not pressure survivors to have an orgasm. In fact, part of the difficulty survivors have in achieving orgasms may be that they are pressuring *themselves* into having one and are thus engaging in frenzied activity rather than slowly and sensuously enjoying the feelings they are having.

Sexual Addiction

A person who needs sex or needs to masturbate several times a day, is unable to feel sexually satisfied despite having had sex or a climax that day or even that hour, or needs sex in order to feel loved or to feel good about himself or herself is probably what is known as a sex addict.

While your partner may insist that she desires sex with you because she loves you so much or because you turn her on so much, the truth may be that her strong sexual drive has little or nothing to do with her feelings for you or even with sex, for that matter. She may, in fact, use sex to push down feelings that are given no healthy outlet, such as anger, anxiety, and fear. Or, she may have learned in childhood that sex can relieve tension, and she may now use it as a stress reducer. As an adult, a sex addict may seek sexual release whenever she is under pressure or is unhappy. Since having sex provides her with only a temporary physiological release and does not solve any of her problems, her demand for sex is continual. Some sex addicts also use sex as a way to feel better about themselves or to feel powerful. The need to feel powerful may have come from the person's having been sexually abused as a child.

Besides demanding frequent sex, the sex addict may also insist that sex always involve "kinky" acts (for example, bondage, flagellation, humiliation, or bestiality). Many male survivors constantly look through porno magazines, watch X-rated movies, or urge their partners to explore alternative life-styles, such as nudist colonies, swingers' clubs, or bisexuality.

Sexual Promiscuity

If your partner is sexually promiscuous, the damage to your self-esteem can be tremendous. Whenever you discover that your mate has been unfaithful, all the understanding and rationalizing in the world will not help you. Although you may understand intellectually and logically that your partner is acting out due to the sexual abuse, and that it has nothing to do with how she or he feels about you, emotionally, you will not really believe it. Having a promiscuous mate will make you doubt your masculinity or femininity, your sexual attractiveness, and your ability to sexually satisfy a mate. As a result of being with a promiscuous survivor, some partners have suffered from sexual dysfunctions.

Knowing that your partner has been with someone else sexually cannot help but cause you to feel devastated and enraged. You will not be able to prevent your body from reacting, no matter how much your mind "understands" that the other person didn't mean anything to her. Emilio, the husband of a survivor who had been extremely promiscuous, told me:

"Each and every time my wife was with another man I would become extremely nauseated and feel like throwing up. She'd try to comfort me, but I couldn't stand to have her near me. She seemed dirty to me, contaminated by the hands of the guy she'd been with. It always took me a long time before I could let her touch me without feeling sick to my stomach, but finally, I guess I let my need to understand outweigh my body's reaction, and I'd be sexual with her again. Now I realize that my body was telling me something. It was not healthy for me to continue having sex with her after these episodes, or to stay with her for that matter. I was going against myself, against my own best interests. I'm in therapy now and repairing the damage of being with her for so long."

In addition to the emotional damage it does to you, being with someone who is promiscuous can endanger you physically, exposing you to AIDS and venereal disease.

TAKING THE PRESSURE OFF

If your partner has a sexual dysfunction of *any* kind, the last thing he or she needs from you is pressure. The following anecdote about a former client of mine, Albert, illustrates how a partner can contribute to a survivor's sexual problems.

Albert was married to a woman who constantly belittled him about ejaculating prematurely. After each sexual encounter she would let him know that he had failed to satisfy her, that she didn't think he ever tried, and that if he didn't start trying she was going to leave him. In desperation, he entered therapy, hoping that this would at least show his wife that he was serious about changing. However, his wife not only did not stop pressuring him, but she actually increased the pressure by constantly asking him how long the therapy would take and making him feel guilty for spending the money.

Albert began to last shorter and shorter lengths of time, until eventually he was ejaculating before penetration. His wife became so impatient and frustrated that she finally refused to have intercourse with him at all and eventually filed for divorce.

During the time Albert and I worked together, he remembered that he had been sexually abused by an uncle when he was a child. The tremendous shame and self-hatred he felt because of this experience had contributed greatly to his prematurity. Interestingly, though, after his wife divorced him and Albert began a sexual relationship with a woman who did not put him down or pressure him, he discovered that in no time he had absolutely no problems at all lasting as long as he wanted.

While his wife had certainly not caused Albert's problems, she had certainly exploited his self-doubt and pressured him so much that he had had no chance at all for overcoming his problem while in that relationship.

One way of taking the pressure off is to do the sensate-focus exercises discussed earlier. These were originally designed as a treatment for sexual dysfunction because they relieve both parties of having to perform and because they teach alternative ways of becoming intimate. There are many other such exercises, some of which were designed for specific sexual dysfunctions. These exercises can be found in any number of books, many of which are listed in the back of this book.

Many survivors despair at ever being able to get over their problems, and many feel depressed and hopeless as more and more time goes by without change. But the situation is far from hopeless. As she progresses in her recovery from the sexual abuse, the survivor's symptoms will lessen and will eventually disappear completely. As she moves through the shame, as she continues to rebuild trust, as her self-esteem increases, and as she is able to learn how to be intimate, she will gradually be able to enjoy healthy sexuality.

ACKNOWLEDGING YOUR OWN SEXUAL PROBLEMS

Survivors often get involved with partners who have their own sexual problems, but because the survivor's problems are so obvious and so pervasive the partner's problems often go unnoticed. Often, a relationship with a survivor is a safe hiding place for those who have sexual problems, because they may not have the demands placed on them that they would in other relationships. While the prosurvivor may complain later on that his partner is not sexual enough or some other such problem, in the beginning of the relationship he may have actually been relieved to learn that she had a rather low sex drive.

This was the case with Riley, who had experienced impotency problems in all of his past relationships and had been humiliated and rejected numerous times. When he met Charlene and she refused to have sex until they were married, Riley felt relieved. He didn't want to risk losing her by once again failing to achieve an erection. To Charlene, Riley seemed to be the most understanding man she had ever met, someone who really loved her for herself and not just for her body.

On their wedding night, Riley attempted to have intercourse with Charlene, only to feel the humiliation once again of being unable to perform. In an attempt to comfort him, Charlene reassured him that it didn't matter to her, and that she didn't really enjoy sex all that much, anyway. She told him that she had been sexually abused by an uncle when she was a child, and because of this she had never really liked sex all that much. Riley felt as if he had been let off the hook, and he didn't attempt to have sex again for several weeks. When he did make an attempt, he was successful, probably because much of the pressure to perform had been removed by Charlene's assertion that she didn't care much about sex.

Throughout the years, Riley was impotent from time to time, but he seldom worried about it. Although Charlene never turned him down, he knew that she had sex just to please him. Nothing was ever again said about Charlene's sexual abuse.

As so often happens, Charlene thought that the abuse was behind her. Her husband seemed understanding about her lack of sexual desire, and she felt blessed with a happy marriage and a comfortable life. After she saw a movie about childhood sexual abuse, however, Charlene's painful memories of the abuse came back to haunt her. She began to cry throughout the day and night, and she became more and more isolated from everyone. She withdrew from her husband and didn't even want him to put his arms around her to comfort her. She could no longer sleep in the same bed with him and began to sleep on the couch. Sex was completely out.

Fortunately, Charlene got into therapy shortly after this and began to recover from the trauma. Several months after beginning therapy she was finally able to sleep in the same bed with Riley and even allow him to hold her. A few months after that, Charlene felt that she was willing to attempt to have sex with her husband once again.

But Charlene didn't want to resume their intimate relationship on the same terms as before. She didn't want to simply "service" her husband but to enjoy sex herself. This meant that she needed Riley to get much more involved with foreplay.

Riley became extremely threatened by Charlene's newfound interest in sex. Suddenly, all his old performance anxiety came back, and his problems with impotency intensified. Instead of realizing that he was now going to need to address his own long-buried problem, Riley began to blame Charlene for his impotency. He complained that she needed too much foreplay, and that by the time she was ready for intercourse he was already turned off.

Riley's pride was at stake. He didn't want to admit that he still had a problem after all these years. It would have been much easier to continue putting all the blame on Charlene, but fortunately, Riley respected how hard Charlene had worked on her own recovery and he didn't want to do anything to jeopardize it. He told me:

"Charlene is the kind of person who always blames herself and I finally realized how terribly unfair it was of me to use this as an out."

With a great deal of trepidation, he admitted to Charlene that he, too, had sexual problems, and that perhaps they could see a sex therapist together. Charlene felt very encouraged by this suggestion and began looking forward to the prospect of their being able to enjoy a healthy, exciting sex life together—which, by the way, they did accomplish.

Difficulties can also arise when one partner is aware that she has been sexually abused and that her sexuality has been affected by the abuse, while the other partner is in denial either about the fact that he or she was also abused or about its effect on the couple's sex life.

In order for Evonne to become sexual with her lover, Celia, she needed to connect with Celia emotionally by having an intimate conversation or by having them spend some time together massaging and caressing each other. Celia, on the other hand, didn't like to massage or caress because she said it aroused her too much, and having a long, intimate conversation with Evonne felt too threatening to her. She said she needed sex *first* in order to connect, and then she would be able to open up emotionally and share her feelings. For months on end, Evonne and Celia went around and around on this issue, both trying to understand the other's perspective and yet each unable to change.

Finally, they agreed to come into counseling. While I was taking their histories, Evonne told me that she had been sexually abused by a trusted friend of the family when she was ten. She connected this trauma with her fear of trusting others and with her need to establish an emotional connection with Celia before they had sex. When I asked Celia if she had ever been sexually abused, she said no.

However, the longer I worked with the couple, the more I suspected that Celia, too, had been sexually abused. First of all, she was very uncomfortable with any kind of sexual foreplay, and even with giving or receiving massages or caresses. Second, she seemed almost addicted to sex, needing it in order to feel lovable. Many survivors felt loved or wanted only when the perpetrator was having sex with them.

As more time passed, I shared my suspicions with Celia and explained my reasoning to her. Finally, she was able to tell us that she had, indeed, been molested as a child by her father, but had never thought it affected her that much. With this disclosure, Celia was able to get the help she needed to recover from her own abuse, and she and Evonne were able to work together to overcome their sexual problems.

In addition to getting involved with those who also suffer from a sexual dysfunction, many survivors also tend to get involved with sex addicts. As mentioned earlier, some survivors are sex addicts themselves and it would follow that these people would gravitate toward one another. But even those survivors who are not very interested in sex seem to be attracted to sex addicts. Since many perpetrators were sex addicts, it makes sense that some survivors would unconsciously develop a pattern of getting involved with those who are like their perpetrator.

If you are a sex addict you may also have been a victim of childhood sexual abuse, been introduced to sex very early in your childhood (perhaps by a child who had already been abused), or, as a child, you may have gotten in the habit of masturbating when you felt upset, angry, or hurt.

Continually pressuring your partner for sex, masturbating obsessively, or steeping yourself in pornography, is damaging not only to your relationship with the survivor but also to yourself. There are Twelve-Step programs for sex addicts and several books written about the subject that will help you understand your problem better and to find ways of controlling it.

Although sexual dysfunction can severely hamper your sexual relationship, there *is* hope. As mentioned earlier, many dysfunctions are merely symptoms of the sexual abuse and therefore subside or disappear entirely as the survivor recovers. Others can be reversed as the couple practices the sensate-focus exercises and as they both learn to take the pressure off. Still other dysfunctions may need the help of a professional sex therapist but are nevertheless curable.

In the last two chapters we have focused on the sexual side of your relationship with a survivor and on the many problems that may arise. In the next chapter we will examine another aspect of your intimate relationship, one that is closely related to sexuality. This is the issue of power in the relationship—who has more of it, what that person does with it, and how it affects the relationship, including the sexual aspects.

Chapter Ten

Power Plays: Who Has More Control in the Relationship?

Survivors frequently attract two extreme kinds of partners: those who control the survivor, or those who allow the survivor to control them. The chances are very high that in your relationship with a survivor, one of you tends to be more dominant and the other more passive. Also, one of you may tend to be abusive in some way, while the other may tend to allow himself or herself to be abused.

In some cases, we are talking about overt, extreme domination and abuse, but more than likely we are talking about more subtle forms of domination and control. While you and your partner may have settled into a rather comfortable and familiar way of dealing with each other, this does not automatically mean that your way of relating has been a healthy one for either of you.

Whether the survivor is the victim or the abuser in the relationship (and sometimes they can be *both*), the relationship may tend to follow a pattern that closely resembles his or her original abuse. Survivors may unconsciously choose partners who resemble the perpetrator both emotionally and physically, often getting involved with someone who is the same age as the perpetrator is or was, in a similar occupation, and has some mannerisms and behaviors similar to those of the perpetrator. Some choose partners who, like the abusive parent, emotionally deprive the survivor, are overly critical, and are extremely controlling or possessive. Or, survivors may find partners who resemble themselves as children, then proceed to treat them as they themselves were treated by the perpetrator. These abusive relationships tend to confirm the survivor's belief that relationships must be abusive.

ASSESSING THE BALANCE OF POWER

Any good relationship is necessarily a relationship of equals. This means that both parties contribute equally to the relationship, and that each is seen as an equal in the other's eyes. In emotionally abusive relationships, there is an inequality of power, with one person feeling superior to the other.

Unfortunately, when one or both partners in a relationship were victimized as children, there is seldom equality in the relationship. One person almost always has more power and thus more control. Since you are involved with someone who was victimized as a child, and since you yourself may also have been victimized, it is very likely that you and your partner have an unequal relationship.

The following questions will help you to examine just which one of you has more power in your relationship. This alone does *not* necessarily establish that you have an abusive relationship. However, answering the questions can help you to spot any inequality that exists. Take some time to think seriously about the questions before you answer them. You may wish to have your partner or friend answer the questions as well.

---

1. *Who has more personal power in the relationship, you or the survivor? That is, who seems to be the stronger of the two, in terms of being able to ask for what he/she wants and being able to take care of himself/herself emotionally?*

2. *Which one of you has a stronger need to be in control? Who usually gets his/her way in terms of choosing what the two of you will do at any given time? Who has control over the finances? Who is more in control of your sexual relationship?*

3. *Which one of you seems to be less satisfied with your partner and with the relationship? Which one of you has more complaints about not getting his/her needs met in the relationship? Which one of you is more critical of the other one?*

4. *Which one of you has more self-confidence? Which one feels better about himself/herself?*

5. *Which of you is more successful in his/her career? Who makes more money?*

6. *Do you think that one of you loves the other more? Who is more emotionally dependent on the other? Which one of you would have a harder time going on without the other one?*

7. *Would you say one of you feels superior to the other one in the relationship? If so, who?*

If you've answered "me" to most of these questions, you have more power in the relationship. It would be abusive of you to use this power to control your mate. If you've answered "my partner" to most questions, you may allow your partner to control or even abuse you.

If You Have More Control

Are you abusing your power by controlling someone who is weaker and thus easily manipulated? Perhaps you unconsciously chose a partner who was weaker so that you could feel powerful and in control. This was the case with Reed, the husband of a survivor:

"I realize now, to my dismay, that I got involved with Pamela in the first place because she seemed so weak and helpless. Being around her made me feel great—I felt so much stronger than I really was. *I* was the one in charge for a change.

"Unfortunately, I didn't realize that after a while I would actually begin to hate her for her weakness, just as I hated myself for my own. I slowly began to misuse my power in the relationship by demanding more and more from Pamela, and becoming more and more critical of her. In the meantime, I wasn't dealing with my own weaknesses and problems but compounding them, because the more abusive I became the less I liked myself."

There are several reasons why you may have become involved with someone who is not your emotional equal:

- You can control the other person or have power over him/her.
- You have low self-esteem, and you don't think a healthier, stronger person would want to be with you.
- Because you are afraid of rejection, you choose to be with someone whom you think is unlikely to reject you, either because she is more needy than you are, or because she has so many problems.
- You can get away with being abusive to the person, because you know he/she will put up with your behavior.
- You are afraid of being alone.
- The other person is a reflection of how you really feel about yourself.
- You are repeating a pattern from your childhood and are treating your partner in the same way one of your parents treated the other one or treated you.

Let's talk in more detail about the last item above. Many of us grew up watching one of our parents dominating the other. For example, you may have seen and heard your father constantly putting your mother down while your mother silently took it. Or, you may have heard your mother constantly complain to your father that he wasn't ever going to make anything of himself, that he was a lazy good-for-nothing who couldn't even support his family properly. Whatever it was that you grew up watching and hearing, your parents were your role models and thus provided you with a picture, however distorted, of what it is like to be in a relationship. It isn't hard to see how early childhood experiences can help shape us and contribute to who we are as adults.

Take a good look at the way you and your partner interact. Are you treating her the way your father treated your mother, or vice versa? From what you know of your partner's parents, does it seem that she is treating you the way one of her parents treated the other?

It is not a coincidence that many partners of survivors were themselves emotionally, physically, or sexually abused as children. If you were abused in any way as a child or if you grew up in an alcoholic or dysfunctional household, you are carrying the emotional scars of your childhood with you today. The abuse, deprivation, or neglect that you suffered damaged your self-esteem, causing you to underestimate your abilities and desirability. It has more than likely caused you to have difficulties with intimacy and closeness in your relationships, and it may have given you a problem with control to the point of being too aggressive.

Many of those who were abused as children, especially males, cope with their abuse by utilizing a form of denial called "identifying with the aggressor." When a young child refuses to acknowledge to himself that he is being victimized but instead justifies or minimizes the behavior of the abuser, he will often grow up to be very much like the abuser, behaving in the same abusive ways. Unfortunately, this is the case with many partners of survivors, as it was with Jacob:

"When I was a little boy, my father, whom I loved very much, would suddenly fly off the handle and slap me or my brother in the face for no apparent reason. Sometimes he slapped me so hard that I fell down, but the most painful part of it was the hurt I felt that my dad could do such a thing. I just couldn't understand how someone who was normally so nice to me could turn on me so quickly. In order to cope with his mercurial behavior, I convinced myself that his behavior was justified, and that I deserved it.

"When I married Gina, I found that I ended up treating her just as my father had treated me. Most of the time I was the ideal husband, but every once in a while I would fly into a rage for no apparent reason, and I would often slap Gina in the face, just as my father had slapped me. And, just as I had justified my father's behavior when I was a kid, I justified my own. I convinced myself that Gina deserved to be slapped because of something she had done. I didn't recognize that I was just repeating the pattern of my father's abusive behavior toward me and my brother."

Survivors of childhood abuse are easy targets for abusers. Because survivors generally have so much shame and such low self-esteem that they feel no one would want them, when someone does pay attention to them, they are very grateful. If the person the survivor becomes involved with ends up being abusive in some way, the survivor is likely to stay in the relationship anyway, either because she is afraid of not finding someone else and of being alone or because she tends to blame herself for whatever happens in the relationship.

If Your Partner Has More Control

Not all survivors tend to be the ones with the least power in the relationship. A common reaction survivors have to their sexual abuse is to become overly controlling and domineering. Because they had so little control during childhood, they tend to overcompensate and now feel they need to be in control of others. Thus, some survivors deliberately choose partners they can control, as was the case with Carla and Robin, who are in a lesbian relationship.

The two had met when Robin was a senior in high school and Carla was in her second year at a junior college. Robin admired Carla tremendously for her popularity and for her artistic talent. Carla was attracted to Robin because she loved being admired, and because Robin didn't pose a threat to her in any way. Since Carla was older, more experienced, more talented, and more popular, she had the upper hand in the relationship right away.

As the relationship developed Carla became more and more domineering, controlling every aspect of Robin's life—from whom she had as friends to what jobs she took. If Robin tried to speak up for herself, Carla would go into a tirade, saying that Robin didn't really love her or didn't trust her to know what was best for her. These comments would tend to confuse Robin, who only wanted to please Carla, much as she had always tried in vain to please her domineering mother.

Robin became more and more unhappy, and she finally talked Carla into going into therapy with her. As I worked with them, it became clear rather soon that Robin was allowing Carla to treat her like a child. It took a while longer for the reasons for Carla's insistence on control to come out. It turned out that she had been very dominated by her father and that he had brutally abused her, both physically and sexually. Carla had vowed that no one would ever control her again. She was finally able to make the crucial connection concerning her treatment of Robin:

"I guess I was so afraid that someone was going to control me again that I made *sure* it wouldn't happen by choosing someone I could control completely."

There are many survivors who tend to get involved with partners who will allow them to be in control or even to be abusive. Just as many partners of survivors identified with the aggressor, so did some survivors. Survivors are fully capable of becoming abusive themselves, whether emotionally, physically, or sexually. Out of touch with their own feelings and with their own victimization, some survivors have unconsciously chosen to play the role of the victimizer in their relationships. Other survivors, extremely angry for having been victimized but afraid to confront their abusers, take out their anger on their partners. Still others have generalized their rage at the perpetrator to include "all men" or "all women."

Joe, the husband of a survivor, told me what it was like to be married to a woman who basically hates men:

"Mary Jane has a huge chip on her shoulder toward men. Unfortunately, I seem to get the brunt of it. She's always calling attention to the things that I do that are supposedly typical of men or 'macho.' She criticizes everything from the way I dress and the way I sit to my sexuality."

Now, Joe is not at all the typical "macho" man. In fact, he is far from it. Raised by a very domineering mother, Joe is actually rather timid and passive. Although he is not effeminate, he does not seem very masculine, either.

"I guess I learned to play down my masculinity even with my mother, because now that I think about it, she discouraged me from being macho, too. I guess you could say that I'm henpecked."

Asked how he felt about having been treated this way by both his mother and his wife, Joe showed some anger for the first time.

"I don't like it one bit. I hate macho men myself, and I would never act that way, but it feels to me like both my mother and my wife want to take away part of my identity. I *am* a man, after all. They've both made me feel like being a man is a bad thing, and it isn't! There certainly are some men who are bad and who are abusive, but I'm not one of them. And I don't want to be abused or to be made to pay for the bad things that other men have done!"

Joe had, indeed, been emotionally abused by his wife for some time, and he was just beginning to realize it. He had married a woman who treated him in the same abusive way his mother had treated him, and he had allowed her to do it because he was so accustomed to it. Joe needed to deal with his anger toward his mother, to learn that he had a right to stand up for himself, and to work on ridding himself of the shame he felt about being a male. Only by doing these things would he be able to stop allowing his wife to emotionally abuse him.

Because of their lack of trust, many survivors are extremely critical, demanding, easily disappointed, hurt, and angered. Suspicious and afraid, they are convinced that people can't be trusted or depended upon; they wait for their partners to do something wrong, then "pounce." Or, they demand so much of their partners and are so critical that they eventually push them away. Through criticism, unreasonable demands, and emotional outbursts, they may wear down their partner's ability to keep trying. This is exactly what happened with Meredith and Bruce:

"Meredith is very, very critical of me. It's as if she expects me to be perfect, and of course I can't be. I feel like I'm walking on eggshells with her all the time. I'm not allowed to make any mistakes, because she always takes whatever I do personally. It seems I'm always hurting her feelings, disappointing her, or making her angry. It's getting so that I'm beginning to doubt myself and my perceptions. Maybe she's right—maybe I *am* insensitive, selfish, and uncaring. I just don't know anymore."

It wasn't long after Bruce told me this that he ended up leaving Meredith, even though he loved her very much. He suffered a deep depression for several months afterward. In one of our sessions during this time he told me, *"I feel like such a failure because all I wanted to do was please her, but I couldn't."*

The sad truth is that some survivors are never pleased by their partners because they are so convinced that people don't really care about each other, that people can't be trusted, that all anyone wants them for is sex, and that relationships are impossible. When one partner has beliefs like this, it is nearly impossible for a relationship to work.

JUST WHAT *IS* ABUSIVE BEHAVIOR?

Because emotional, physical, and sexual abuse are so common in relationships between survivors and their partners, it is important that you understand exactly what abuse entails so that you can better ascertain whether you are being abusive or being abused. Often, we are being abused or abusive without realizing it. We all have a tendency to deny our own or a loved one's abusive behavior. However, facing the truth will set you free, for it is only when you admit that there is a problem that you have a chance to change things. The following descriptions of abusive behavior can help you to recognize your own or your partner's abusive behavior, perhaps for the first time.

If you find that you are either being abusive or being abused, don't judge yourself too harshly. Remember that the chances are very high that you were either abused as a child or that you observed abusive behavior in your formative years and are thus repeating a pattern. Sometimes, just discovering that we are repeating such a pattern can help us to break it.

Emotional Abuse

There are many ways to abuse someone without laying a hand on him or her. Read the following paragraphs carefully and honestly to determine whether you are guilty of being emotionally abusive or if you are being emotionally abused.

Domination

There are many ways to dominate others. You can insist on always getting your own way and on making all the decisions, by not allowing the other person to have an opinion or to speak his or her mind, or by threatening rejection or even physical violence if the other person does not comply with your wishes. When you dominate another person you are in a sense enslaving her and depriving her of autonomy.

Verbal Assaults

This type of behavior involves berating, belittling, criticizing, name calling, screaming, threatening, blaming, and using sarcasm and humiliation. This kind of abuse is extremely damaging to the victim's self-esteem and self-image. Just as assuredly as physical violence assaults the body, verbal abuse assaults the mind and spirit, causing wounds that are extremely difficult to heal. It is also important to remember that if you are a male who is verbally assaulting a female, you are also intimidating her with the unspoken threat of physical violence, and this is extremely frightening.

Unreasonable Expectations

It is abusive to place unreasonable demands on another person, such as expecting that she put aside everything to satisfy your needs, demanding her undivided attention, requiring that she spend all her free time with you, or demanding that she submit to sex whenever you want it. It is also abusive to be dissatisfied no matter how much she gives and to criticize any attempt she makes to please you.

Emotional Blackmail

Emotional blackmail means either consciously or unconsciously coercing another person into doing what one wants by playing on that person's fear, guilt, or compassion. Emotional blackmail is one of the most powerful ways of manipulating another person. You are using emotional blackmail whenever you threaten to end the relationship if your partner doesn't do what you want, or when you reject your partner or distance yourself from her until she gives in to your demands.

Unpredictable Behavior

If your partner experiences you as unpredictable because you have drastic mood swings, sudden emotional outbursts for no apparent reason, or inconsistent responses, you are being emotionally abusive to her. You are also abusing your partner with your unpredictable responses when you react very differently at different times to the same behavior from your partner, telling her one thing one day and the opposite the next day, or liking something one day and hating it the next. Those who abuse alcohol or drugs are often extremely unpredictable, exhibiting one personality when sober and a totally different one when intoxicated or high.

This kind of behavior is abusive because it forces the other person to constantly be on edge, never knowing what to expect from you. She must remain hypervigilant, always waiting for your next outburst or change of mood. Living with someone whose behavior is unpredictable is tremendously demanding and anxiety provoking, causing the abused person to feel constantly frightened, unsettled, and off balance.

Constant Criticism

When you are unrelentingly critical of your partner, always finding fault and never being pleased, you are being extremely emotionally abusive. Over time, this type of abuse eats away at your partner's self-confidence and sense of self-worth and undermines any good feelings she has about herself and her accomplishments or achievements. Eventually, she will become convinced that nothing she does is worthwhile, and she may feel like just giving up.

Character Assassination

When you humiliate, criticize, or make fun of your partner in front of others, discount her achievements, constantly blow her mistakes out of proportion, talk openly about her past failures and mistakes, or tell lies about her, all in an attempt to discredit her or make her look bad in the eyes of others, you are guilty of character assassination. This behavior obviously causes your partner to feel a great deal of pain and embarrassment and can damage her self-esteem tremendously. In addition, it damages her reputation, causing her to feel isolated and insecure socially and even professionally.

Gaslighting

This term comes from the movie *Gaslight,* in which a husband used a variety of insidious techniques to make his wife doubt her perceptions, her memory, and her very sanity. When you deliberately and continually deny that certain events occurred or deny that you said something when you know you did, or when you insinuate that your partner is exaggerating or lying when you know she isn't, you are playing a very malicious and dangerous game.

Constant Chaos

When you constantly cause upheaval and discord, when you deliberately start arguments and are in continual conflict with your partner, you are being emotionally abusive. You may not be consciously intending to bring about constant chaos but may be "addicted to drama," having grown up in a dysfunctional, highly chaotic, or alcoholic family where there were frequent arguments, physical abuse, or other forms of disruption or upset. Having grown accustomed to a tremendous amount of change, violence, and crisis, you may actually be addicted to the excitement created when there is conflict, or you may not know of any other way to be. You may even become depressed and anxious when life is stable and uneventful and only feel truly alive after you have survived a threatening or highly charged experience.

Physical Abuse

Any physical show of force for the purpose of intimidating, threatening, or controlling another person is physical abuse. Physical abuse can include slapping, hitting, punching, shaking, kicking, pushing, tripping, burning, biting, pinching, or hair pulling. Other acts of physical abuse include throwing objects at the person or using an object to hit her, banging her head against something, holding her down, forcing her to sit or lie in a certain position, or forcing her arms behind her back.

You do not have the right to physically abuse your partner, no matter what she has done to you. Similarly, she does not have the right to physically abuse you. It has been estimated that 50 percent of American women have been physically abused by their husbands or lovers. Many of these women were victims of physical, sexual, or emotional abuse when they were children.

Men can also be physically abused by women, although this does not occur as often as the other way around. Men who are physically abused by their female partners are also likely to have been abused as children. Because they have damaged self-esteem, a fear of being alone, and a feeling that they deserve to be mistreated, these men often put up with the abuse and do not fight back even though they may have the physical strength to do so.

Physical abuse also occurs in gay and lesbian relationships, with the inequality of power often being emotional rather than physical.

Sexual Abuse

Some survivors get involved with partners who abuse them sexually in much the same way that they were abused as children. (Or, conversely, they may sexually abuse their partner.) Sexually abusing your partner can damage her severely. Such abuse may take a variety of forms:

> ➤ Pressuring a survivor into having sex by continually harassing her.

The term *sexual harassment* is used most often with regard to work settings, but a woman or man can be sexually harassed by anyone, including a lover or spouse. Sexual harassment is defined as unwelcome sexual advances or physical or verbal conduct of a sexual nature. Whenever you pressure your partner into becoming sexual against her will, you are sexually harassing her. This is especially damaging to a survivor of childhood sexual abuse, who was pressured to become sexual when she wasn't old enough to do so and forced to perform sexual acts against her will.

If a survivor says she doesn't want to have sex but you won't take no for an answer, instead attempting to "change her mind" by trying to arouse her, trick her, make her feel guilty, or do anything else to coerce or manipulate her, you are doing exactly what the perpetrator did. While she might eventually become aroused if you touch her long enough, she will feel used and manipulated afterward. Or, she may give in out of guilt but then feel angry and resentful toward you.

You are also pressuring and manipulating your partner if you threaten to leave her or withdraw your love if she doesn't have sex with you or participate in certain sexual acts. This also falls into the category of emotional blackmail, discussed above.

➤ Physically forcing the survivor to have sex against her will.

Physically forcing someone to have sex is rape. This is true even if the person is your spouse or lover. When your partner says no or doesn't consent to sex and you force yourself on her anyway, you are guilty of rape.

➤ Pressuring the survivor into engaging in sexual acts that she finds distasteful or repulsive.

If you suggest a type of sexual activity but your partner expresses a lack of interest or is turned off to the idea, drop it. It is abusive for you to hound her or try to make her feel guilty for not doing what you want. Survivors are often turned off to certain sexual acts because it reminds them of their earlier abuse.

➤ Treating the survivor as if she were a child or "play acting" that she is a child and you the adult.

While being playful during sex can be a very fun and healthy thing to do, pretending that one of you is a child and the other is an adult is abusive to a survivor. It is a replay of the sexual abuse she or he sustained as a child and should be avoided at all times. This includes talking baby talk, wearing diapers, or having the survivor dress in children's clothing.

➤ Pressuring a survivor to watch pornographic movies, look at pornographic magazines, or read pornographic literature.

Many child molesters introduced their victims to pornography as part of the sexual abuse. Because of this, survivors are often repulsed and sickened by pornography of any kind. Pornography is also very often a depiction of a woman being used, degraded, or forced to have sex. For this reason, when a survivor watches or reads pornography it often has the effect of reabusing her. Male homosexual pornography often has a "victim" and a "perpetrator" and can also involve acts of sadomasochism and bondage, which may be a replay of the abuse the male survivor experienced.

- Pressuring a survivor into "kinky" sex, such as group sex, sadomasochism, and bondage.

While you may feel curious about some of these things and interested in trying them, they will more than likely turn the survivor off, since once again it is likely to remind her of the sexual abuse. If your partner has said no to your requests and you continue to pressure her, you run the risk of having her be resentful of you or completely turned off to you, or of having her give in and then be traumatized by the experience.

Healthy sexual relationships require that both people feel equally powerful, and that both are freely consenting to any sexual activity engaged in.

To avoid the possibility of sexual abuse in your relationship with a survivor, adopt the following rules:

- No force (not even "fantasy rape")
- No sadomasochism
- No bondage and discipline

Sexual abuse of a child causes a connection to be formed in the child's mind between sex and shame, sex and anger, sex and power, and sex and control. Breaking these connections is a major goal of recovery for survivors.

Any sexual activity or even a reference to sex can cause a survivor to feel shame. You are therefore asking for trouble when you bring in such things as fantasy rape, sadomasochism, fetishes, bestiality (having sex with animals), urolagnia (urinating on your partner or having your partner urinate on you), and so on.

You will need to make sure that sex with your partner is not a game on your part, a way for you to release your anger or to make yourself feel powerful or in control. This is what the perpetrator did.

Kurt, the partner of Ted, a male survivor, told me how he and his lover had become aware that they were reenacting Ted's abuse:

"I had always had a strong need to be in control, so I would choose people who were weaker, who seemed to need me to be in charge. Ted seemed to feel comfortable having me be in control, having me be the boss, so our relationship worked for a long time. But when I learned that Ted had been sexually abused by his older brother, I began to feel squeamish about always being the dominant one. I started feeling as though I was abusing Ted, even though he liked my dominance. It got so bad that I started having trouble getting erections.

"We went to therapy together, and we found out that we had been re-creating Ted's abuse by his brother. I had actually been doing the same things to him that his brother had done. Even though this had always turned Ted on, we both realized that we had to stop doing these things. Otherwise, it was just too sick. It took us a while, but we were finally able to make some significant changes in our lovemaking so that Ted wasn't constantly being reabused."

Sex with a survivor needs to be an honest expression of love, affection, caring, and sensuality or playfulness. If it is anything else—a power trip, an ego builder, a tension releaser, an addiction, or a way to avoid other problems—it will feel bad to the survivor and will repeat the abuse she suffered as a child.

Also, you cannot allow yourself to play the role of an authority figure, parent, or abuser, even if both of you are aroused by this role-playing and even if it is the survivor who initiates it. It is a replay of the sexual abuse, and it is unhealthy for both of you.

WORKING TOGETHER TOWARD A HEALTHIER RELATIONSHIP

While your lover or mate certainly does have obvious problems, problems that affect the relationship, you need to be aware that you, too, have problems that may also affect the relationship. Whether you have sexual problems of your own, problems with intimacy and trust, or a tendency to be abusive, you need to look at and work on your own issues if the relationship is to be a strong and healthy one.

Continue to look at your own behavior for signs of dominance and submission. While it will be difficult, catching yourself when you are being abusive or controlling or when you are allowing your partner to abuse or control you, can help you to change your patterns of behavior little by little. For some, seeking professional help may be the answer, since changing patterns rooted in childhood abuse can be a very difficult process.

The most important thing is to be honest with yourself so that you can come out of any denial you have about your behavior. You and your partner can then work together toward a more equal—and more satisfying—relationship.

Chapter Eleven

Should You Stay, or Should You Leave?

Even though you may be working on your part of the relationship problems, paying attention to your own abusive or passive behavior and to the balance of power in the relationship, your partner may still be too caught up in her own recovery to focus on her part of the relationship problems. Out of necessity or out of habit, many survivors continue to focus on themselves and their recovery to the point that the relationship has truly disintegrated. Or, you both may be doing the best you can, working hard on changing negative patterns, yet you remain at an impasse.

It is inevitable that your relationship with the survivor will go through a transition during the survivor's recovery. Sometimes people go through this transition and come out the other side far closer than they have ever been. This is especially true when both the survivor and the prosurvivor are working on themselves and are both growing and changing. Because they have shared so much pain and growth together, survivors and prosurvivors often find that they have created an extremely strong bond, one that makes them capable of withstanding any future hardships.

On the other hand, some couples discover that both partners have changed so much that they no longer have very much in common. They may find that they have been staying together out of obligation, or because they are afraid of being alone. This is exactly what Maureen, the wife of a male survivor, realized:

"During my husband's recovery it became evident that we had been clinging to each other out of insecurity and fear, not out of love. I don't know now whether we ever really loved each other—at least, in a mature way. We got together as teenagers. I think we got married partly because of sex, and partly because we were both afraid to leave home and face the world alone."

In some cases, one partner outgrows the other. This is most often the case when the survivor has been working on herself, while her partner has been focusing so much attention on the survivor that he has not spent enough time on his own growth. Dustin, a new client of mine, discovered this after his wife had already left him:

"After all the time I spent supporting Tracey, after all the years of sacrifice, the first thing she did when she got better was to leave me. I couldn't believe it. I had thought that by standing by her all that time I was guaranteed to have a wife who would be eternally grateful and who would never leave me. Boy, was I surprised! Now, I realize that I should have been spending more time working on myself. The fact is, she outgrew me. She had become extremely aware of herself because of her therapy, and I was still where I was when we first got married. She could no longer relate to me, nor I to her, but I was so insecure I would have held on forever anyway."

Sometimes, a couple finds that their growth as individuals has taken them in separate directions, as Teri explained:

"During the whole time my husband was focusing on his recovery, I was working on furthering my career. Now we find that we have very different values. I feel it is important to provide our children with financial security and the best education money can buy. My husband, on the other hand, doesn't think money is important at all. He feels that the most important thing we can do for our children is to spend quality time with them.

"Since I now make so much more money than my husband, he has suggested that he stay home and be the primary parent to our children. I know this has worked out for some people, but frankly, I just can't respect a man who doesn't work and make at least as much money as I do. He thinks I am just too materialistic. Maybe I am, but I've worked long and hard to get where I am, and I feel good about myself. I want my kids to have the same opportunity I had. I don't think my husband and I are ever going to see eye to eye, and I find myself becoming attracted to some of the men at work who share my way of thinking. And I think my husband would be better off with someone from one of his Twelve-Step programs, someone who is as involved with personal growth as he is."

Trevor and his wife, Mia, also grew in different directions:

"Mia was really damaged as a child. Not only was she sexually abused by a teacher, but she was also neglected terribly by her mother. I guess I was pretty screwed up myself when we first met, because my childhood wasn't so great, either. But the more therapy I got, the stronger I became. My wife became stronger in some ways, too, but her strength seemed to lie in her becoming more independent from me. Instead of her becoming more loving as time went by, she became more and more distant. I realize now that she probably needs to be alone for a while to develop a sense of identity separate from me. I don't know if she'll ever truly love me. It just didn't feel healthy any longer for me to continue waiting for someone to learn to love me."

IS THIS RELATIONSHIP WHAT YOU WANT?

Whatever your particular situation, at some point you and your partner may need to assess your relationship almost as if it were a new one, with both of you having to decide whether it makes sense to continue with it. Because the recovery process can be so long and difficult for both the survivor and the prosurvivor, it is normal to sometimes wonder whether or not you are with the right person. In the following pages, you'll find several questions to ask yourself to help you determine whether you and your partner should stay together. You may wish to write your answers down and even share them with your partner.

> ➤ What do you want in a relationship? Describe the kind of relationship you really want, trying to be as realistic as possible.

Lenny, the husband of a survivor, wrote the following description of what he was looking for in a relationship:

"I want a relationship in which both people work together to make both of their lives as rich and rewarding as possible. I want us both to have our own separate lives, too, so that we can each grow to be the best we can be, but I want there to be a real sense of togetherness—not the "joined-at-the-hip" togetherness you so often see, but more of a silent commitment to each other and a real joy at being together."

After writing this, Lenny realized that he and his wife, Patty, did have what he had described as his ideal relationship:

"We really are a team. Sure, it gets hard sometimes, but I always feel as though we're working together. We want the same things out of life, and we have the same values. We like many of the same things and we do give each other a lot of space to explore our separate interests."

Thinking about the kind of relationship you want may make you keenly aware that your present relationship is not what you want at all. Corey, the boyfriend of a survivor, wrote:

"I want a relationship filled with passion and excitement, where we stay in bed making love for hours and only get up when we have to. I want to take off for long romantic weekends and to spend vacations traveling to exciting places. I see life as an adventure, and I want someone who feels the same way, who wants to soak up all that life has to offer."

After Corey wrote this, he realized that he and his girlfriend, Paula, were not even close to having this kind of relationship.

"Paula hates to stay in bed with me. When we do have sex, it's short and sweet, and then she wants to get up and do something else. As for traveling, she hates to leave home, where she feels secure. We've never had a good vacation yet. She always starts fights and by the time she's adjusted to a new place it's time to come home.

"I love Paula, but I guess not enough to sacrifice years of my life. She's always in so much pain. I don't know how long it will take her to recover, and even then I'm not sure if she'll ever really like sex."

➤ What is your ideal sexual relationship?

As reflected in Corey's list of most desirable traits in a partner, sexual compatibility is certainly an important issue to consider. It is especially important to discover what each other's concept of the ideal sexual relationship is. Write down the answers to the following questions and have your partner do the same:

➤ Ideally, how often would you like to have sex?
➤ Which sexual activity do you enjoy the most?
➤ What is your idea of the most exciting sexual scenario?
➤ What kind of sexual activities would you eventually like to engage in?
➤ What kind of sexual activities are definitely not something you want to engage in?

Use your lists as a starting point for a heart-to-heart discussion about your sexual relationship. During your discussion, you may discover that your partner may never want to engage in some of the sexual activities that you are interested in. This may merely be a question of sexual preference or it may be that certain sexual acts will always remind her of the sexual abuse. While recovery is certainly possible for survivors, the recovery process is similar to that of recovering from a major operation. A survivor's wounds can be healed but there will always be scars and memories of the trauma that may influence her sexuality. For this reason, it is important to know just where each of you stands in terms of sexual preferences and needs. For example, perhaps oral sex is something that you definitely want to have as a part of your sexual relationship but your partner expresses a strong dislike for it. It would be unrealistic for you to assume that once she has recovered, she will suddenly discover a strong interest in oral sex. While it is possible that she may become more tolerant of it, she may never really enjoy it. This means you will either need to adjust to this reality and not push for oral sex, or honestly ask yourself whether you will be truly satisfied in a relationship with little or no oral sex.

- What kind of person do you most value?

Following is the list that Selina, who is married to a male survivor, wrote in response to this question:

- Someone who is honest both with himself and with others.
- Someone who is able to make a commitment to a relationship, who can be faithful and dedicated to making a relationship work.
- Someone who treats me with respect and treats me like an equal, not as someone who is subservient to him.
- Someone who is caring, kind, and generous.
- Someone who wants a family and who will make a good father to his children.

After writing this list, Selina realized that her husband was everything she had ever wanted.

"I couldn't believe that I had actually described him. Because things have been so hard for so long, I guess I lost track of what a truly wonderful man he is, until I looked at my list. I'm lucky to have him!"

➤ Do you and your partner share common goals for the future?

Write down some of the goals you hope to achieve in the next few years, and ask your partner to do the same. Your goals may be very specific, such as saving money to buy a new house, or they may be more general, such as continuing to grow.

Compare your lists of goals. Do you share very many goals, or do you seem to have entirely different ones? After reading your partner's goal list, do you find that you would like to add some of his or her goals to your list? If so, recognize this as one measure of how much you and your partner have in common.

WHEN IS ENOUGH ENOUGH?

While most survivors do not intend to hurt their partners, they may end up doing so. Many of the coping behaviors survivors have adopted are destructive ones, such as sexual promiscuity, alcohol and drug abuse, overeating or starvation, a need to always be in control, and sometimes even abusive behavior. While you may understand that the survivor you are involved with cannot help her destructive or abusive behavior, you cannot be expected to tolerate it when it is damaging to you or to your children.

If your partner is an alcoholic or a drug abuser who refuses to get help, you may need to end the relationship for your own welfare. Untreated, these diseases will bring nothing but chaos into your lives and can endanger both your partner's life and your own. As long as the survivor is using alcohol or drugs to hide from her feelings and memories, she has little chance for recovery.

No one will be able to tell you how long you should wait, how long you should keep trying with a survivor. You will need to decide this for yourself, and the decision will likely be a difficult one.

THE DECISION TO LEAVE

Not all relationships can withstand the strain of the recovery process, with its ups and downs, its tensions, and its high emotional intensity. You may have already put a lot of time and effort into a relationship that doesn't seem to get much better, or gets only slightly better, over time. Because your partner is so damaged by the sexual abuse, she may be unable to give you the affection, nurturing, and support you deserve. You just don't think you can continue the relationship because it hurts too much—it hurts to have the one you love not return that love, it hurts to be continually blamed for something that you didn't do, and it hurts to have your love distrusted and doubted. There may come a time when you reach the sad conclusion that it is far too damaging to you to stay with the survivor any longer, and that you need to choose yourself, and your emotional well-being, over the relationship. This was the conclusion that Murray, the boyfriend of a survivor, was finally forced to come to:

"I kept thinking that things were going to start getting better any time. But as soon as we'd get through one crisis or one phase of recovery, there would be something else to focus on. I've come to the conclusion lately that I can't keep going on with it. I care about her, but as long as I'm with her I don't think I'll ever really deal with my own issues enough. The temptation to focus on her issues is just too great, and she demands a lot of my time and energy. I feel as though I need to give some time and energy to myself for a change."

You may have learned to take better care of yourself and have as a result decided that remaining in the relationship is not in your best interests. You may have realized that you were a codependent or a caretaker when you entered the relationship, hiding from your own feelings by focusing on your partner's problems. You may have learned to be much more independent and so do not have a need to be in a relationship for the main purpose of not being alone. Or, the survivor's behavior may be damaging to you or to your children. Several prosurvivors who decided to leave explain their decisions to do so:

Lena, the friend of a female survivor:

"I guess I just got to a place where I valued myself much more than I ever had before, and I felt I deserved a lot more than I was getting in this relationship."

Wilma, the wife of a survivor:

"After I'd been working on my own issues in therapy for quite some time, I began to realize that I'd always chosen someone who had severe problems, and that this was a way for me to avoid my own. But after a while this started getting old. I didn't get my own needs met because I was always meeting someone else's. I guess I got healthy enough to realize that I was sacrificing my own happiness to take care of someone else, someone who probably didn't even really love me."

Les, the husband of a survivor:

"I knew that Melanie had been hurt very badly by her father and mother, so I tried to make up for all her pain by being really good to her. Unfortunately, as time went by I began to realize that she just couldn't take in my kindness. She had been treated so cruelly for so long that all she could focus on were the times when I *didn't* treat her as well as I could. I became very depressed in the relationship because no matter how hard I tried it was never enough, and no matter what I gave it wasn't the right thing. Finally, I just had to leave because the relationship was just not healthy for me."

Erica, the wife of a survivor:

"I knew it was time to leave when my husband began to be seductive with our daughter. He denied it, of course, but I saw all the signs—the way he looked at her, the way he was always holding her on his lap and touching her legs and buttocks. I knew he had been sexually abused and I felt sorry for him. I wanted to stand by him while he went through therapy but I couldn't risk my daughter's emotional well-being. I knew the best thing for all of us was for me to tell his therapist about my observations, and then to insist on sole custody of our daughter with no visitation rights until he could be trusted to be with her."

Good Reasons to Leave:

Your partner is sexually abusing your child.

Your partner is unable to be faithful to you.

Your partner's problems are interfering with your career.

Your partner's problems are damaging your physical or emotional health.

Bad Reasons to Leave:

Your partner is spending too much time in therapy and at groups.

Your partner isn't getting well fast enough.

You feel your partner is changing too much, and you want things back to the way they used to be.

Your partner is becoming too assertive.

If you decide that for your own best interests you need to leave the relationship, recognize that this does *not* mean you have failed somehow. The time you have spent with the survivor has undoubtedly been very valuable for both of you, and has certainly not been a "waste of time." You have both learned a great deal about yourselves, and you have undoubtedly shared many good times.

Choosing to be in a relationship should be a voluntary commitment for both partners, not one that is based on guilt, shame, obligation, or fear of being alone. Both you and your partner have been under a great deal of stress because of the sexual abuse. While you have probably both tried as hard as you can to make the relationship work, neither of you can perform miracles. Ultimately, each person must decide what is best for himself or herself, and sometimes this does mean a separation or a termination of the relationship.

THE DECISION TO STAY

Every relationship has problems; this is a given. In your relationship with the survivor, you know what these are and how to cope with them. You've come a long way with this person already and have invested a lot of time in working on the problems. Leaving this relationship would *not* mean that you will not have to deal with new problems in your next relationship; these are inevitable. Looking at your current situation from this perspective may help you to see things in a more positive light, like these prosurvivors:

"Being with Ruth is certainly difficult at times, but as long as she's working on her problems in therapy I have hope. Besides, I know that all relationships have problems. Getting involved with someone who wasn't molested seems like a great idea at times, but then I realize that I might be in for worse problems—who knows? At least with Ruth I know what I'm dealing with, and I know there will eventually be an end to it."

"Sometimes I think about leaving Sam, because struggling day after day with the same issues gets so hard. I fantasize about being involved with someone who doesn't have all these problems, and it sounds great. But then I remember all the other men I *have* been with, and that they all had things about them I didn't like. I remind myself that there is no perfect man or perfect relationship. I think about how hard Sam works on himself and how honest he is about his feelings, and I come away once again with a deep respect for him. I've been around enough to know that *everybody* has problems, no matter how perfect they may seem at first, and that most people don't work on themselves like Sam does."

Good Reasons to Stay:

You have seen some real progress on the survivor's part.

Your partner has started therapy or a Twelve-Step program.

Your partner has stopped blaming you for all the problems in the relationship and has now acknowledged that many of your problems as a couple stem from her sexual abuse (for example, her lack of interest in sex and her difficulty in trusting you).

Bad Reasons to Stay:

You're afraid of being alone.

You feel that your partner owes you something after all this time, and you want to stick around long enough for her to pay her debt.

You have control over someone else.

If you decide to stay, you will undoubtedly be called upon to continue growing and changing. Aaron, the husband of a survivor, reflected on his relationship with his wife and on his own growth:

"Because Dawn's father controlled her and was so possessive of her, she really insists on having her own life, separate from mine, and on being her own boss. I hated this at first, but now I realize it's been really good for me, because I tend to be both too clingy and too bossy. I've had to learn to trust that she will always come back to me, and that she'll end up doing what's right for her and for the relationship. I've had to work on becoming much more independent since I've been with Dawn, and I like myself a lot better because of it. I've never known a relationship like this before, one with such equality and give-and-take."

WHATEVER YOU DECIDE . . .

Whether you decide to continue your relationship or to end it, you will have benefited from the experience of being with a survivor. One of the many benefits is that you have likely discovered a lot of things about yourself that you never knew, opening doors to your own further growth.

During his relationship with Wendy, a survivor, Eugene discovered that he, too, had been sexually abused as a child:

"When Wendy and I first became involved, I had no idea that I had been sexually abused. But during our relationship, as I watched her go through the pain of remembering her abuse and listened to her talk about what had happened to her, I began to suspect that I had been abused, too. There really was no other explanation for the intense way I was reacting. Finally, my own memories came back, and I realized that I *had* been molested.

"Wendy and I went through our recovery together, and it was by far the most important period of my life. Because I was with her, my whole life has changed."

In your relationship with a survivor, you may have discovered that you became involved with this person for your own unhealthy reasons, as discussed earlier. Even if the relationship ends, know that you will benefit tremendously if, for the first time, you are able to walk away from a relationship that is not healthy for you.

Many prosurvivors, inspired by the courage and determination of their partners, have found the courage through the relationship to face their own problems. This was the case with Leeanne:

"Carl really works on himself—in therapy, in his Twelve-Step program, and writing in his journal. I admire him so much for it, and it's really encouraged me to be the best I can be, too. He's come so far, considering the horrible childhood he had. I feel so proud of him, and I want to be as proud of myself. Since I've been with Carl I've become far more honest with myself about my own problems. For one thing, I admitted that I am an alcoholic and have joined AA—something I probably wouldn't have done if I hadn't been with someone like Carl."

A THANK-YOU TO PROSURVIVORS

The best way I can think of to end this book is to share with you a letter and a list that were written by survivors to their mates, acknowledging their support throughout the recovery process. While your friend or lover may or may not be able to write you such an acknowledgment, rest assured that she or he feels the same way about you as these survivors did about their prosurvivor partners.

> Dear Adam,
>
> I would like you to know how very grateful I am to you for being there for me all during my recovery. I know how hard it was for you to sit by and let me cry, even though you wanted to hold me and make all the pain go away. I know how hard it must have been for you to let me scream and holler and hit the bed, since you hate violence of any kind. And honey, I sure know how hard it was for you to go without sex all those months, being the little sex hound that you are.
>
> You truly have been my port in the storm throughout my recovery. I always knew you were there, even though I may not have acted as if I cared sometimes. And knowing that you were there, that you were standing by, kept me going even when I was tempted to throw in the towel.
>
> All my love,
> Amelia

Hilary wrote this thank-you to her best friend, Andrea:

> Dear Andrea,
>
> I want to thank you for being such a support to me during my recovery from the sexual abuse. I couldn't have hoped for a better friend. You were the first person I told and the first person who believed me. I still remember how angry you got at my father and how validated that made me feel for being angry myself. You were always the first person I thought of calling when I felt depressed or afraid and you always dropped what you were doing to listen to me.
>
> Andrea, I don't know if I could have gone through this ordeal alone but I am sure grateful I didn't have to. You are the best friend anyone could hope to have and I hope that now that I am feeling stronger I can be there for you if you ever need me. God bless you.
>
> Love,
> Hilary

Another client, Marta, wrote a thank-you list to give to her mate:

- Thank you for holding me while I cried.
- Thank you for understanding when I couldn't have sex.
- Thank you for taking over so many of the responsibilities when I was so out of it.
- Thank you for not complaining about the amount of money I was spending on therapy.
- Thank you for working together with me on our relationship problems and on being able to admit when you had a problem, too.
- Thank you for being such a good parent to our children so I didn't have to worry about your molesting them.

Chapter Twelve

Self-help Groups for Partners

by Jan Myers

As the partner of a survivor, you may not have thought of joining or starting up a self-help group of your own. Having read this book you may feel that most of your questions have been answered and your problems addressed. However, if you feel that you'd like to talk to another person in the same situation as yourself, this chapter suggests how you might find other partners in an already existing group or how to start up your own group.

Jan Myers is director of ***Self Help Nottingham****, an organisation working with individuals and groups to promote and develop self-help. Jan Myers has worked in the voluntary sector for over fifteen years and has had much experience of working with survivors.*

Partners of survivors receive little help in coping with the difficulties of living with an adult recovering from childhood sexual abuse. Yet their relationship with the survivor will be affected and both the partner and the relationship can suffer. Often the survivor is both in therapy and a self-help group, yet it may not have occurred to her or her partner that a support group would be helpful to the partner. In a support group the partner could benefit from talking to others in a similar situation about their mutual experiences and ways of coping with them.

What follows will provide you with basic information about self-help groups generally and will give you specific information on starting your own group for partners of survivors. But remember; self-help groups are not a cure-all. They are not a replacement for individual counselling or therapy.

What's the difference between self-help groups and therapy or professionally-led groups?

Self-help is one way in which people find help in coping with crises such as bereavement, disability, changing life circumstances, childhood sexual abuse. The power of self-help is that the members are responsible for how the group is run and controlled. In therapy or support groups this power ultimately lies with the trained therapist or group leader and the helper and helped are not always inter-changeable. The professional facilitator will retain the job of helper in therapy and support groups.

Often self-help groups grow out of professionally guided groups. They continue to meet, without a professional facilitator, to support their members over a longer period of time. They are a complement to professional care.

Benefits and limitations of self-help

Groups can provide members with much needed information and act as a sign post to other services and support. For people with long term medical conditions, for example, groups can improve members' knowledge of the illness and ways of coping. Stress and emotional upset can be reduced. Groups often involve sharing each others' difficulties and sadness. Opportunities can also be created for people to talk about the good things in their lives. They are places for fun, friendship and a sense of belonging. They can raise people's confidence, their self-esteem and their feelings of self-worth.

Yet, self-help groups are not for everyone. Some people prefer the closeness of one-to-one therapy rather than collective experience. In some groups, a high turnover of members can cause instability within the group. Others may attend meetings without committing themselves to the group or its aims.

Finding an existing group

Although there are many carers groups and associations in the UK, there is very little for partners of survivors of sexual abuse. The groups which do exist are called Co-dependents Anonymous. These are a particular type based on the 'Twelve Step Programme' and the traditions of Alcoholics Anonymous. The twelve steps are to do with admitting you have a problem and asking yourself searching questions. There are twelve steps groups in most major towns and cities in the UK.

Co-dependents Anonymous members will not only include partners of adults from sexually abusive situations. They may have family members or partners who have alcohol or drug dependency problems or where primary relationships are dysfunctional. Often members can also belong to other twelve steps groups such as Alcoholics Anonymous, Al-Anon, Narcotics Anonymous, Overeaters Anonymous or Sex and Love Addicts Anonymous. If there is a group in your area, you may want to visit to see if it meets your needs. Often groups like this will have open evenings when new or potential members can visit.

Starting your own self-help group for partners

By visiting other self-help groups as well as twelve steps groups, you can get an idea, for example, of how different groups work, the size of their membership and the activities they undertake. You can decide whether a twelve steps programme is appropriate, or whether you want a more formal/informal gathering. You can discover some useful hints and suggestions and avoid some of the common pitfalls. If you decide to start a twelve steps group then it is best to contact the regional or national organisation. These types of groups have a definite structure. Members follow a programme of moving through twelve steps to recovery. They produce their own information and guidelines on running groups.

Take time to consider whether you want to start a group. You will have individual needs which may or may not be met in this way. However, the organisational issues and questions for a partners group are likely to be no different from any other self-help or carers group.

What do you want the group for?

By asking yourself this question, you can start to think how best your aims can be achieved. For example, if you are in a same sex relationship you may want to work with other lesbians and/or gay men. There could be particular cultural issues or issues around racial discrimination which may make it more meaningful for you to have support from within the Black community. You may feel that, despite different issues, there are many common themes across genders and cultures and you want the group to be able to address all of these needs.

Your membership of a self-help group is entirely voluntary and should be based on the benefit you feel being a member will provide. This can be as simple as meeting with people with similar issues on a regular basis. What you want to achieve from participating can also determine how you organise and structure your activities. It will also help you to deal with issues of membership and participation.

Size

Self-help groups can be any size - from two people to twenty-two or more. In order to discuss personal and intimate details, it may be appropriate to control the numbers of people attending the group. If your aims are to raise awareness generally and increase information about the problem, then larger numbers of people attracted to open meetings with specialist speakers could be organised. If offering a telephone contact point for people at a time of crisis is considered more important than face to face meetings, a larger membership and training for people who would be willing to operate such a service will be needed.

Does it suit your needs to have an open group where members can come and go and where there are likely to be different people at each meeting? Or will it be more beneficial for you to have a closed group with a smaller number where the same people attend each meeting? Closed groups have found that between six to twelve people is a good size to work well yet give a feeling of continuity and safety for members.

Organisation and decision making

Spend time thinking and planning before you meet. It is never easy to deal with relationships in groups and thought needs to be given to all the positive and challenging things that might come up.

Consider things that you will be able to deal with, those for which you may need support and those that you feel are not within the boundaries of the group. If you intend to set up a small group, try to work these guidelines out within the group as a whole. If you want to attract a larger more fluid membership, have a planning group of about four or five to start to think about these things.

In the initial stages, some groups need the influence of a strong individual to take it forward. However, the long term effect of good leadership is to help other people to learn and to take responsibility. Think about the jobs that can be shared in the group. This could be keeping a record of members, recording any decisions or making sure the room is booked for meetings. Each person can also work with another group member so that skills are passed on. This helps the groups to remain intact if one or more key members leaves.

Good facilitators can help to make the meeting run well. Facilitators are members of the group who help it to run smoothly although they do not have more power than other members. They can help to encourage quieter members, or pacify an anxious or overly talkative one. They work to encourage other people to make the most of their time and help the group to achieve its aims in the meeting.

Groups go through different stages of development. Once people get to know each other better, they feel more confident about airing differences in opinion. There might be power struggles over what different people feel is the best direction to take. Working through these difficulties together can help a group become stronger and more cohesive.

Keep some kind of written records, or a scrapbook of events and photographs, over the lifetime of the group. This helps to celebrate the group's existence and its achievements. Record any significant decisions and ground rules. It can be used as a reference to clarify misunderstandings or to challenge people's behaviour.

Ground rules need to be decided by the whole group and written down. They can include agreements on the way people can act or behave towards each other; for example:

- Respect other people's time to speak - we should not talk over people.
- Confidentiality - everything that is said within the group stays within the group.
- Challenge our behaviour but not us as individuals.
- Everyone should try to be on time for each meeting.

If someone consistently talks over someone else or does not let a person finish what they are saying, any member should feel comfortable in challenging them. You might say "We all agreed that we should not talk over other people. Do we still want to keep this as a rule or do we need to change it?" If everyone is aware of the basic principles, then each person can have a role in contributing to the smooth running of the group. A feeling of equality among members also makes communication easier.

Having clear aims and objectives at the start will help you to evaluate how well a group is performing. Remember that aims and objectives are not set in stone and, as needs change over time, they can be revised accordingly. This kind of regular evaluation can also help when attracting new members. They will be aware of what the group plans to achieve and therefore able to choose whether or not to be involved.

Getting people together

Getting people together is probably one of the most difficult tasks for a new group. If there is a national organisation, contact them to see if they can offer any help. Similarly, in many towns and cities there are local development agencies such as Councils for Voluntary Services to help you in just this kind of activity. Some have self-help development workers. In rural areas, rural development councils or parish community centres can be approached for help. If your partner is a member of a group, he or she may know of others who would be willing to start a group. Think carefully about where and how you find like-minded people.

You may want to carry out some planned publicity e.g. small posters or leaflets. Again, think carefully. You may not want to include personal details such as a name and address or telephone number. A self-help centre or Council for Voluntary Service could give you a mail box or act as an initial contact point for you. In this instance, any publicity you produced would need to make it clear that enquiries were through a third party. Be clear about whom you are trying to attract - in this instance people to start a new group. Too much publicity too early can bring a huge amount of attention from potential members, as well as from counsellors and other professionals. It can raise expectations beyond the initial scope of a new group, especially if there are no other similar resources in your area.

How often to meet and where?

In the first year, many groups can move around and juggle with meeting times and days before settling on a consistent time and place. Some meet regularly e.g.: "every Monday 7.00 p.m.-9.00 p.m.". Others meet monthly or six weekly. Others meet only when the need arises and members keep in contact by mail, telephone and, now, by e-mail and internet groups. You may decide in the early stages to meet regularly, even once a week. As the group develops this could be harder to sustain. Needs may change and it may become more realistic to meet monthly.

Finding a convenient and accessible venue can take some searching. In the planning stages, it will be cheaper and easier to meet in someone's house or to rotate meetings between members' houses. Here you will need to think about the impact on others in your household and the cost of the meeting, even if only in terms of providing tea, coffee and biscuits.

Think also about the impression given to potential members. Often it can be easier to arrive at and enter a neutral meeting place. This may be preferable to one that can suggest that existing members have a friendly and cosy relationship. There are ways around this of course. For example, an existing member can arrange to meet a new member before a meeting - perhaps for coffee and a chat - to explain what the group is about and what it does. The new member will then have a familiar and welcoming face if they decide to come along to a meeting.

The size and layout of a room can also make a difference to how your group works. Sitting shivering in a large church hall will not help a small group of five or six to speak openly or easily. A smaller room, with comfortable chairs in a circle or semi-circle may be better. By seeing everyone else, discussion and thoughts can be shared. Think about the less obvious things too, such as lighting, flowers perhaps and tissues as well as the practical issues of how people will find you. If the room is on a first or second floor is there a lift for people who may have mobility problems?

Money matters

Often, with small groups, little funding is required; enough to rent a room, buy refreshments or purchase resources such as useful books and leaflets. Later as the group becomes more established money may be needed for other things: to publish posters or leaflets or to pay for visiting speakers. It is best to get advice from a local Council for Voluntary Service or Community Accountancy Project for information on raising and looking after money. They will also be able to point out any legal requirements associated with fund-raising.

Outside help

How much do you want to do yourself and how much do you feel could be done by other services providers such as counselling centres, health and social services? Think about the relationships you will want to build with people and organisations outside the group. Many of the twelve steps groups like Co-dependents Anonymous are entirely autonomous and have no connection with external agencies.

Remember to use your members' own networks. If people are able, and willing, to act as ambassadors, they may be able to attract support from different sections of the community. If you are clear about how you might want to link in with people from outside the group, you can also be clear about saying no to unwanted offers of help.

Increasingly, many more health and social care professionals are aware of and appreciate the value of self-help activity. Many groups have built up strong and mutually beneficial relationships with relevant professionals.

Self-help development workers are available in different parts of the UK to help support you in your activity. There are also small groups workers and community development workers employed by Councils for Voluntary Services and some local authorities. Some can help to provide you with training and ideas on running a group successfully. They often help with initial publicity and meeting space and can signpost help and support from other agencies.

If you are in one-to-one counselling or therapy, you can talk to your counsellor about your ideas. They may be able to help you to get in touch with others in a similar situation by displaying a small poster on their noticeboard. They may also know of contacts in other locations that you can visit for ideas, or be able to recommend books, tapes and videos.

Building up accurate and up-to-date information on other services and groups is vital. It is inevitable that at some point someone will contact the group or want to join when it is obvious that the group will not meet their needs. In this instance, you will want to put them in touch with a group or professional who can help them.

Issues to think about

An effective group will have a high level of trust and an ability to cope with decision making and problem solving. One of the key issues in developing trust is safety within groups and in particular the issue of confidentiality.

Groups are more likely to flourish when members feel sure what they say is not going to be repeated outside the meeting. This is particularly the case when members know and meet each other and each other's families in situations outside the group. Every group decides exactly what is right for them although there should always be an agreement on confidentiality. This can also include exceptions to the rule too.

Some survivors have dropped out of their support groups because their partners felt insecure about the amount of time and energy they gave to the group. Others continued because of the support they received. This would be an issue for partners groups too.

Groups can provide an appropriate and safe place to voice fears, feelings of rejection or impotence and anger. Group members can discover and share ways of discussing issues in a positive way. A member of a co-dependents group described her group as "wonderful" because she received "unconditional support" and "unconditional hearing" from other members.

Communication is not just about talking to each other. It is also about being aware of how we support and comfort each other and about being open enough to question ideas and resolve difficulties. Take time to get to know each other and each other's needs. If someone is angry or upset, do they like to leave the room accompanied by another group member? Is it enough to hold their hand or sit closer to them?

Often conflicts are part of poor communication between members. For example, someone in the group may be struggling to comprehend how their partner could have allowed abuse to occur, or why she did not tell him earlier in their relationship. Other members may already have dealt with this situation. The first member could feel that the others just do not understand; similarly other members may feel that he is being negative and so blocking his inability to move on. By taking time out to examine the gap and allow both sides to communicate, the first member can receive support in coming to terms with his own feelings. The group can also maintain its cohesiveness and move on at an appropriate time.

A number of books which deal with the issues of group dynamics will be available in your local library. Councils for Voluntary Services also have small resource rooms where they keep information relevant to small groups.

What's in it for you?

Becoming part of a self-help group may give you a better understanding of yourself generally. Feeling more secure in yourself can heighten your awareness of your own emotional needs. This in turn can make you more supportive of your partner. Your relationship may become more balanced as each of you finds support through your journey of self-discovery. You may be fulfilled by being able to help someone else. You may get lots of help yourself. You may make many new, supportive friends. And, you could find yourself doing all sorts of things you never dreamed you could do. Your life could be changed completely and for the better.

AA – Alcoholics Anonymous (twelve steps)
PO Box 1 Stonebow House,
Stonebow,
York YO1 2NJ
Tel: 01904 644 026

British Association of Settlements and Social Action Centres (BASSAC)
Provides resources and help for self-help community initiatives.
1st Floor, Winchester House,
11 Cranmer Road, London SW9 6EJ
Tel: 0171 735 1075
Fax: 0171 735 0840

CoDA UK – Co Dependants Anonymous
Ashburnham Community Centre
Tetcott Road,
London SW10 OSH
Tel: 0171 376 8191

Community Network
Provides telephone conferencing facilities to charities and not-for-profit organisations. Up to 10 people at a time can join in on one telephone conversation and no special equipment is needed. There are Community Network centres in London, Birmingham, Manchester, Inverness and Belfast.
2nd Floor, 50 Studd Street,
London N1 0QP
Tel: (head office) 0171 359 4594
Tel: (bookings) 0171 704 0404

MIND: National Association for Mental Health
There are locally based MIND organisations.
Granta House, 15-19 Broad Way,
London E15 7RJ
Tel: 0181 519 2122
Fax: 0181 522 1725

National Association of Councils for Voluntary Service (NACVS)
There are over 230 CVS throughout England.
3rd Floor, Arundel Court, 177 Arundel Street, Sheffield S1 2NU
Tel: 0114 278 6636
Fax: 0114 278 7004

National Council for Voluntary Organisations (NCVO)
Provides information, training, legal, advisory and membership services for national voluntary organisations.
Regent's Wharf, 8 All Saints Street, London N1 9RL
Tel: 0171 713 6161
Fax: 0171 713 6300

Northern Ireland Council for Voluntary Action
Co-ordinates and develops voluntary action in Northern Ireland
127 Ormeau Road, Belfast BT7 1SH
Tel: 01232 321 224
Fax: 01232 438 350

Scottish Council for Voluntary Organisations
Co-ordinates and develops voluntary action in Scotland.
18/19 Claremont Crescent, Edinburgh EH7 4QD
Tel: 0131 556 3882
Fax: 0131 556 0279

Self Help Nottingham
20 Pelham Road
Sherwood Rise
Nottingham NG5 1AP
Self-help groups, information, support, development
Tel: 0115 969 1212 information enquiries
Tel: 0115 969 1514 general enquiries
Fax: 0115 960 2049

Sia
National development agency for the black voluntary sector.
Winchester House, 9 Cranmer Road, Kennington Park Road, London SW9 6EJ
Tel: 0171 735 9010
Fax: 0171 735 9011

Telephone Helplines Association
The aim of the Association is the assurance of the highest quality response for all those seeking information, advice and help via the telephone.
61 Grays Inn Road, London WC1X 8LT
Tel: 0171 242 0555
Fax: 0171 242 0699

Wales Council for Voluntary Action
Co-ordinates and develops voluntary action in Wales.
Llys Ifor, Crescent Road, Caerphilly, Mid-Glamorgan CF8 1XL
Tel: 01222 869 224
Fax: 01222 860 627

Bibliography

Survivors

***Beginning to Heal*: A first Guide for Female Survivors of Child Sexual Abuse**
Ellen Bass & Laura Davis
Cedar, New York, 1993
An introduction to the healing process, for women just beginning to recover from child sexual abuse.

***Breaking Free*: Help for Survivors of Child Sexual Abuse**
Carolyn Ainscough & Kay Toon
Sheldon Press, 1993
Information about sexual abuse and practical suggestions for overcoming the effects of abuse.

***The Courage To Heal*: A Guide For Female Survivors of Child Sexual Abuse**
Ellen Bass & Laura Davis
Cedar, New York, 1988
A handbook with information about many aspects of sexual abuse, and some self–help exercises. Written for women but helpful for men too.

***The Courage To Heal Workbook*: For Women and Men Survivors of Child Sexual Abuse**
Laura Davis
Harper & Row Publishers, New York, 1990
Checklists, open-ended questions, exercises, art projects and activities.

***The Healing Way*: Adult Recovery From Childhood Sexual Abuse**
Kristin Kunzman
Hazelden Foundation, USA, 1990
Written for women by a counsellor with experience of addiction and abuse counselling.

I Never Told Anyone
Edited by Ellen Bass and Louise Thornton
Harper Perennial, New York, 1983
Writings by women survivors of child sexual abuse.

I Know Why The Caged Bird Sings
Maya Angelou, Virago, 1984
The first volume of Maya Angelou's autobiography. When she was eight years old she was raped, and didn't speak for the next three years.

***The Memory Bird*: Survivors of Sexual Abuse,** Ed. Caroline Malone, Linda Farthing & Lorraine Marce
Virago, 1996
An anthology, made up of hundreds of contributions from survivors of sexual abuse.

***Rescuing The Inner Child*: Therapy for Adults sexually abused as children**
Penny Parks: Souvenir Press, 1990
The book includes exercises and a question and answers section.

***The Right To Innocence*: Healing the Trauma of Childhood Sexual Abuse**
Beverly Engel, M.F.C.C.
Ivy Books, New York, 1989
A therapeutic seven step self-help program for men and women, including how to choose a therapist and find a support group.

Staying OK
Amy and Thomas Harris
Arrow Books, 1995
A book to help sort out three "voices" - "damaged parent", "damaged child" and "adult".

Partners, family and friends

***Allies In Healing*: When The Person you Love Was Sexually Abused As A Child**
Laura Davis
Harper Perennial, New York, 1991
For partners, as well as extended families and therapists.

Families and How to Survive Them
Robin Skynner, John Cleese
Mandarin, 1993
A general book on family therapy. Lots of cartoons and a light touch.

Families In Recovery
Beverly Engel
Lowell House, 1994
Offers support and empathy plus valuable information to help family members cope with the news of sexual abuse.

***Ghosts In The Bedroom*: A Guide for Partners of Incest Survivors**
Ken Graber, M.A.
Health Communications Inc, Deerfield Beach, USA , 1991
A Twelve Step approach to help partners of survivors cope with their own feelings, support the recovery of their partner, and solve relationship problems together.

***Outgrowing The Pain Together*: A Book for Spouses & Partners of Adults Abused As Children**
Eliana Gil, Ph.D.
Dell Publishing, New York, 1992
The book explains the effect of abuse and gives an overview of the healing process.

Self help groups and Counselling

Counselling Adult Survivors of Childhood Sexual Abuse
Christiane Sanderson
Jessica Kingsley Publishers, 1991
Gives an overview of the literature on theories of sexual abuse, its impact and long-term psychological consequences and an examination of different models of treatment.

DABS National Resource Directory
Directory and Book Services,
79 Copley Road, Doncaster,
South Yorkshire, DN1 2QP
Covers services for women, men, children, parents and workers for recovery from and prevention of child abuse. DABS also have a book catalogue.

Handbook of Counselling in Britain
Edited by Windy Drydon and David Charles Edwards
Routledge, 1997

In Our Own Hands
Sheila Ernst, Lucy Goodison
Womens Press Ltd, 1981
A book of Self Help therapy from bodywork to psychoanalytically - based therapies.

Self Help Alternatives to Mental Health Services
Vivien Lindow
MIND Publications, 1994
Practical ideas for service user groups to start their own outreach projects, co-operative businesses, clubs etc.

Starting Off
Self Help Nottingham
20 Pelham Road, Sherwood Rise, Nottingham NG5 1AP
Information and ideas for new self-help.

***Surviving Child Sexual Abuse*: A Handbook For Helping Women Challenge Their Past**
Liz Hall and Siobhan Lloyd
Faloner, 1993
A practical handbook for people working with survivors.

***Survivors Directory* Support Services for Survivors of Sexual Violence in Britain and Ireland**
Broadcasting Support Services
Westminster House
11 Portland Street
Manchester M1 3HU
National organisations, local organisations, specialist services and booklists arranged alphabetically by county.

***Talking It Out*: A Guide to Groups for Abused Women**
Ginny NiCarthy, Karen Merriam, Sandra Coffman
Seal Press, Seattle, USA 1984
Covers the practical details setting up a group for women survivors.

***Who Can I Talk To?* The User's guide to therapy and Counselling**
Judy Cooper and Jenny Lewis,
Headway, 1995
Guide gives an overview of the various therapies and counselling services available in the UK.

Resources

AXIS
Roy Fletcher Centre
12 – 17 Cross Hill
Shrewsbury SY1 1JE
Tel: 01743 357 777
Helen Rogers,
Director of Services
A counselling service offering information, understanding and support to anyone who is in a close relationship with a survivor of childhood sexual abuse.

British Association For Counselling
(BAC), 1 Regents Place
Rugby TZ21 2PJ
Tel: 01788 578 328
Information will be sent to callers on the availability of psycho- therapists, counsellors & other professional bodies. Send A5 SAE.

CASA
(Counselling for Adult Survivors of Abuse)
PO Box 6552, Edmonton
London N18 2SN
Tel: 0181 345 6688
Ms. Fenton, Mr Brennan
One-to-one, groups, talks, training and advice on sexual abuse issues for adults (male and female).

Child Abuse Advisory Service
61 Station Road
Hurlingham Chambers
Clacton On Sea CO15 1 SD.
Tel: 01255 435 000
Counselling for young adult survivors and their families.
Service for offenders also.

Child Abuse Survivors Network
P.O.Box 1, London N1 7SN
Tel: 0171 278 8414
No helpline but newsletter and referral service.Send an SAE for a list of organisations that can offer professional help.

Clapham Common Clinic
151 – 153 Clapham High Street
London SW4 7SS
Tel: 0171 627 8890
No fax service available
Counselling, psychotherapy, relationship counselling for survivors and their partners.

Derby Rape Crisis
P.O.Box 142
Derby DE1 2HF
Helpline: 01332 372 545
Tel: 01332 342 255
No fax service available
Women who have suffered rape or sexual abuse and support for their friends and partners.

Edinburgh Rape Crisis Centre
PO Box 120
Brunswick Road
Edinburgh EH7 5XX
Tel: 0131 556 9437
Includes support to women survivors of child sexual abuse, contact by telephone, letter or face-to-face.

Emerge
The Foundation
Corporation Street
Stafford ST16 3AG
Helpline: 01785 225 991
Individual Support.
Support group for male and female survivors of sexual abuse.
Support group for partners and non-abusing parents.

I.S.A.S.
(Incest and Sexual Abuse Survivors)
85 Millgate
Newark On Trent
Nottingham NG2 4HA
Helpline: 01636 610 314
Tel: 01636 610 313
Counselling for adult survivors, their partners or supporters and parents of abused children.

Institute of Family Therapy
Clinical department
24-32 Stephenson Way
London NW1 2HX
Tel: 0171 391 9150
The Institute offers a service to families and couples in distress, including help to adult survivors of child sexual abuse and their partners.

Life Story Therapeutic Centre
17 Eldon Square
Reading
Berkshire RG1 4DP
Tel: 01189 958 0806
Shen, Dave, Sue, Debbie
Life Story offers counselling and psychotherapy to children, adolescents and adults living with the effects of physical, emotional and sexual abuse be they survivors, partners or relations.

Limerick Rape Crisis
11 Mallow Street
Limerick City
Helpline: 00353 6131 1511
Maura Tobin, Co-ordinator
Counselling offered to male and female survivors. Counselling and support for relatives and partners of survivors.

London Rape Crisis Centre
PO Box 69
London WC1X 9NJ
Helpline: 0171 837 1600
Tel: 0171 916 5466
Trained advisors
Telephone service run by women and girls who have been raped or sexually assaulted at any time in their lives. This free confidential support is open to relatives and friends.

Making Connections
C/O CACS
Second Floor
Queensway House
Essex Street
Southend
Essex SS2 5TD
Tel: 01702 619 414
Robbie Holloway
Produces support newsletter, containing innovative papers, information and articles on current issues relevant to Adult Survival of Childhood Abuse, for workers, allies, survivors.
Instigated by persons participating or involved with the Diploma Course 'Working with Adult Survivors of Childhood Abuse'.

Maudsley Hospital and the Institute of Psychiatry
Maudsley Hospital
Denmark Hill
London SE5 8AZ
Tel: 0171 703 6333/ 0171 919 2371
(Answer 24 hours)
Dr Michael Crowe,
Consultant Psychiatrist.
Providing effective, short term and focussed therapy for individuals and/or couples with relationship or sexual difficulties.

Mind Information
Granta House
15–19 Broadway
London E15 4BQ
Tel: 0181 522 1728
Trained volunteers answer phone enquiries.
Can put the survivor in contact with a number of organisations.

The North London Centre for Group Therapy
138 Bramley Road
Oakwood
London N14 4HU
Tel: 0181 440 1451
Mrs Lesley Holmes, Administrator
Supervision, Support Groups and Workshops.

Offcentre, Hackney Young Peoples Counselling Services
25-27 Hackney Grove
London E8 3NR
Tel: 0181 986 4016/
0181 985 8566
Provides confidential counselling, therapy and group-work for 13-25 year olds who live in Hackney.
Provides specialist support for young people who have suffered sexual abuse.

Pathways
38 Waterloo Road
Epsom KT19 8EX
Tel: 01372 743 338
Counselling for individuals,couples and groups.

R.A.S.A.S.C.
Rape and Sexual Abuse Support Centre
P.O. Box 383
Croydon
CR9 2AW
Helpline: 0181 239 1122
Tel: 0181 239 0099
Women survivors, Self-help groups for women.
People who need to talk about what it is like being the partner of a survivor.

Rape Crisis Centre
PO Box 53
Glasgow G2 1YR
Tel: 0141 331 1990
(voice & minicom)
The Rape Crisis Centre offers free and confidential support and information to women and girls who have been raped, sexually assaulted and/or sexually abused, no matter when or how.
Also provides information and support to friends and relatives and those working with survivors.

Reachout
3 Broadfields Parade
Glengall Road, London HA8 8TD
24 hour helpline : 0181 905 4501
Confidential help and advice for adults who have suffered abuse in childhood, those experiencing domestic violence and their family and friends. Newsletter and handout sheets available on receipt of an A4 sae, postage £1.

RELATE
Herbert Gray College
Little Church Street
Rugby
Warwickshire CV21 3AP
Tel: 01788 573 241
RELATE bookshop at the above address, or local RELATE Centre for counselling.
RELATE centres provide couple counselling for those with relationship problems, psychosexual therapy, relationship education.
Local Centres are listed in telephone directories under 'RELATE' or 'Marriage Guidance'. Specialist bookshop with range of helpful literature.

Samaritans
Tel: 0345 90 90 90
24 hour service. Listening service for people who are in distress.
Alternatively look in the yellow pages for your local branch.

Sandwell Rape Crisis
P.O.Box 2223
West Bromwich B70 8AH
Helpline: 0121 525 9981
Tel: 0121 525 9835
Sally Neath, Centre Manager
Free confidential counselling. Drop in centre for female survivors.

Spectrum
7 Endymion Road
Finsbury Park
London N4 1EE
Tel: 0181 348 0196
Counselling offered to individuals and couples. Family therapy available.

Survivors (Sheffield)
PO Box 142
Sheffield, S1 3HG
24 hour ansaphone: 0114 279 6333
Counselling and support service for men abused as boys, men raped as adults and male partners of victims of rape or abuse.

Survivors of Sexual Abuse
Open Door Project
1-2 Hanworth Road
Feltham, Middlesex
Tel: 01784 210 661
Jeanne Stroud
One to one counselling, helpline, partners' and carers' group.

Survivors' Network
CMHC
79 Buckingham Road
Brighton BN1 3RJ
Helpline: 01273 720 110
Office: 01273 203 380
Hazel Urquhart, Co-Ordinator
Helpline, drop-in, newsletter, individual counselling and groups for women sexually abused in childhood.
Helpline provides information and support for partners, carers, friends etc of women sexually abused in childhood.

Tavistock Centre
Adult Department
Hampstead
120 Belsize Lane
London NW3 5BA
Tel: 0171 435 7111
General psychotherapy service which includes couples therapy for survivors and partners of abuse.

Threshold, Women's Mental Health Initiative
14 St Georges Place
Brighton BN1 4GB
Tel: 01273 622 886/01273 626 444
Providing information and services for women including counselling and drop-in service.

Women's Therapy Centre
10 Manor Gardens Holloway
London N7 6JS
Tel : 0171 263 6200
Individual and group psychotherapy.
Service for women who experience childhood sexual abuse. Fees on a sliding scale.

Women's Therapy Link
P.O.Box 2704
London NW5 2LN
Tel: 0171 916 0123
Counselling and psychotherapy for individuals and couples.